The Visions, Revelations and Teachings of Angela of Foligno

The Visions, Revelations and Teachings of Angela of Foligno

A MEMBER OF THE THIRD ORDER OF ST FRANCIS

Selected and Modernised by
MARGARET GALLYON

THE *Alpha* PRESS

BRIGHTON • PORTLAND

2 4 6 8 10 9 7 5 3 1

First published 2000 in Great Britain by
THE ALPHA PRESS
PO Box 2950
Brighton BN2 5SP

and in the United States of America by
THE ALPHA PRESS
5804 N.E. Hassalo St.
Portland, Oregon 97213-3644

British Library Cataloguing in Publication Data
A CIP catalogue record for this book is available from the British Library.

Library of Congress Cataloging-in-Publication Data
Angela of Foligno, 1248?–1309
[Liber de vera fidelium experientia]
The visions, revelations and teachings of Angela of Foligno : a member of the Third Order of St. Francis / selected and modernised by Margaret Gallyon.
p. cm.
Includes bibliographical references
ISBN 1–898595–33–X (pbk. : alk. paper)
1. Mysticism—Catholic Church. I. Gallyon, Margaret, 1923– II. Title
BV5082.2A54 2000
248.2'2—dc21   00-041601

Printed by Biddles Ltd, Guildford and King's Lynn
This book is printed on acid-free paper

Contents

CONTENTS

Preface

In the early part of the twentieth century Evelyn Underhill, an eminent
authority on Christian mysticism, expressed her surprise that at a time
when there was a revival of interest in St Francis of Assisi and the
Franciscan movement, so little attention was being paid to the thirteenth
century Franciscan mystic, Angela of Foligno. 'Yet,' she added,
'excepting only Bonaventura, this woman has probably exerted a more
enduring, more far-reaching influence than any other Franciscan of the
century which followed the Founder's death . . . Her book of visions,
now so little read, profoundly affected the religious life of Europe.'[1]

Happily today there is a resurgence of interest in the female mystics
whose lives and writings are being re-examined and studied from new
perspectives. Angela of Foligno, a notable Franciscan mystic, is one of
those mystics whose visions, revelations and teachings abundantly deserve
renewed study so as to bring benefit to contemporary readers. On first
discovering Angela's writings the present author was immediately struck
by the wide-ranging and universal nature of her visions, and by the deep
wisdom and perceptiveness of the teachings and letters of instruction to
her disciples.

The purpose of this present book is to provide the general reader
with a selection of Angela's visions and teachings which I have drawn
from *The Divine Consolations of the Blessed Angela of Foligno*, translated into
English by Mary G. Steegman, from a 1536 Italian version.[2] Because the
English of Mary Steegman's translation is now somewhat dated and
contains many obsolete phrases, unnecessary repetitions and lengthy

[1] Evelyn Underhill, *A Franciscan Mystic of the Thirteenth Century*. British Society of
Franciscan Studies. Ex Series 1911.
[2] *The Divine Consolations of the Blessed Angela of Foligno*. Translated from the Italian
by Mary Steegman. Chatto & Windus, 1909.

sentences I have modernised the English to suit present-day readers. I have also removed many of the divisions, sub-divisions and endless numberings which characterise so much of medieval writing, including the steps which Angela took on her spiritual journey.

Speaking of the Italian version from which Mary Steegman made her translation, Fr Algar Thorold, in his introduction, says of this little spiritual masterpiece, 'It is one of the rarest books in the world, and has a special value as being one of the earliest popular devotional works printed in the vernacular in Italy. It takes its place with the *Dialogue of St Catherine of Siena and the Little Flowers of St Francis* among the attempts to popularise mysticism.'

If one compares the Italian version with the earlier Latin version of the visions one finds that the two are essentially the same, and that the differences are minimal, unimportant and peripheral, compared to the spiritual quality, profundity and grandeur of the visions, revelations and teachings.

Because this book is primarily a devotional one, it is suggested that it be read piecemeal, a paragraph, a page or two at a time, and not straight through, thus allowing time for meditation and reflection.

My sincere thanks are due to Dr Saskia Murk Jansen of Robinson College Cambridge for reading the manuscript and offering constructive and helpful comments. My thanks are also due to Chatto & Windus for permission to use Mary Gertrude Steegman's translation of the 1536 Italian version of *The Blessed Angela of Foligno* (1908), which was published as a volume in the New Medieval Library.

In hoc signo vinces.

Libro vtile ꝗ deuo

to nel quale ſi contiene la coñuerſione, pe
nitentia, tentatione, dottrina, viſioni, &
diuine coſolationi della beata Ange
la de Foligni, ncuamente tra,
dutto de latino in lin,
gua volgare

1536

Illuminatiõe fatta alla.B.Angela.
viue in lui,& chi non:& mi disse in veri
ta che non e altra via dritta,cha quella chi
seguita li miei vestigi: per che i questa via
non casca inganno,& questa parola in ve
rita & gráde chiareza, piu volte & in mol
ti parlari mi fu detta. Amen.

Finiscono le visioni & consolationi
della beata Angela de Foligni.

Omnes sta   in corporé
bimus an/   gesserimuf
re tribunal   siue bonũ
Christi, re/   siue ma /
cepturi qd   lum,&c.

Qué genuit, adorauit.

Partus, integritas difcordes tempore lógo

Virginis i gremio, fœdera pacis habét.

The Visions, Revelations
and Teachings of Angela of Foligno

The Book of the Divine Consolation of The Blessed Angela Da Foligno. MDMIX.

The Life of Angela of Foligno

Angela was born in about 1248, twenty-two years after the death of Francis of Assisi, the saint on whom she modelled her life. Her parents were of wealthy Umbrian stock. References in her writings provide evidence of the atmosphere of luxury and extravagance in which she grew up, married and had her children. She speaks of personal vanity, colouring, braiding and adorning her hair, of sweet and delicate foods, of idleness and wastefulness of money, of being 'a slave of vices and iniquities . . . full of greediness, gluttony and drunkenness'. Yet all the time she was making an outward show of being abstemious and observing fasts and austerities.

Foligno, the town of her birth, was set in the beautiful valley of the river Topino in the province of Umbria in Central Italy. It was on this gentle landscape of fields, olive groves and vineyards that she was to gaze in later years while on pilgrimage to Assisi and to hear God speaking to her 'Behold and see! This is my creation!'

In Angela's day the memory of Francis was still fresh in many people's minds. He had received a call from Christ while praying in the little church of St Damian. 'Francis, go and repair my church, which as you can see is all in ruins.' It was to the markets of Foligno that Francis travelled, bearing a load of cloth to sell to obtain the money for the repairs to the church. But it was not only the ruined church of St Damian that he was to restore, for as his biographer, St Bonaventura explains, 'The chief purpose of the message concerned the Church of Christ which he had purchased with his own blood.'[1]

Francis had renounced worldly wealth, rank and possessions and

---

[1] St Bonaventura, *The Life of St Francis*, ch 2. Everyman's Library, 1941.

had literally applied to himself the command of Christ to the rich young ruler of the Gospel. "Go, sell everything you have, and give to the poor, and you will have riches in heaven; then come and follow me."[2] By his gentleness, humility, and profound love for Christ, he was to breathe new life into an ailing Church and to found a movement which was to spread throughout Italy, Europe and to many parts of the world. His followers, few at first, rapidly increased in number, and for these men he formulated a simple Rule based on the life and teaching of Jesus, a Rule which received the official recognition of Pope Innocent III.

A Second Order of Franciscans was founded for women, led by the lady Clare, and a Third Order for lay people. This Third Order, or Order of Penitents as it was originally called, was composed of men and women from all walks of life, married and single, who continued to pursue their ordinary secular occupations while simultaneously binding themselves to the observance of a simple Rule based on the Franciscan ideals of simplicity, poverty, almsgiving, penitence and prayer.[3]

It was to this Third Order of St Francis that Angela of Foligno belonged and her membership of the Order gradually brought about a marvellous transformation in her life, which began with a profound awareness of her sins. This awareness prompted her to pray to St Francis that he would guide her to a confessor to whom she could unburden her conscience. The next day she found her uncle, the devout friar, Arnaldo, preaching in the church in Foligno, and at once she recognised in him the priest to whom she must make her confession. From then onwards Arnaldo became her confessor, adviser and the amanuensis to whom she dictated her visions and revelations.

Like other married women mystics – Margaret of Cortona, Bridget of Sweden and Elizabeth of Hungary – whose spiritual gifts flourished after the death of their husbands, Angela's gifts also flourished after a succession of deaths in her family, all of which seem to have occurred within a short space of time. This makes one surmise that the deaths were the result of one of those devastating epidemics that erupted sporadically throughout the Middle Ages, and which sometimes carried off entire

[2] Mark 10:21.
[3] John Moorman, *A History of the Franciscan Order*, ch 1. Oxford University Press, 1968.

families. The first to die in Angela's family was her mother, who, she says, was a great obstacle to her in following the way of Christ. Shortly afterwards her husband and all her children died. She twice mentions the great grief she felt at the time of their deaths, but she also states that, because she had begun to follow the way of Christ and the cross, she had prayed that if God willed she might be free of them, and that consequently when they died she felt consoled.

This apparently callous attitude of Angela towards her family requires some explanation if the reader is not to be prejudiced against her from the start. First we should note that her conviction that in order to follow Christ she must forsake everything, family, friends, possessions and even her own self, indicates that she had in mind one of the hard sayings of Jesus: 'If anyone comes to me and does not hate his father and mother, wife and children, brothers and sisters, even his own life, he cannot be a disciple of mine.'[4] Here Jesus is asserting the absolute priority of claim which he has upon his followers and Angela is applying the saying to herself. As Ann Stafford comments 'She was an all-or-nothing person and her readiness to sacrifice every family tie, every friendship, every penny, for love of God, expressed her acceptance of, and readiness to cooperate with, his grace.'[5] Evelyn Underhill however observes in this regard that family affection was not the strongest point in the character of the mystics and that 'St Francis himself flung his family aside without scruple when it came to the parting of the ways, and Angela was but following in his footsteps.'[6]

At some time following her religious experiences and confession to Friar Arnaldo, Angela went on pilgrimage to Rome and Assisi, the pilgrimage to Assisi being an event of critical importance to her and contributing to her establishment as a true visionary and mystic and notable religious teacher, which earned her the illustrious title of 'Magistra Theologorum'. It was during this pilgrimage 'on the narrow road which leads up to Assisi, and is beyond Spello' that she heard the Holy Spirit addressing her and exhorting her to love him, assuring her of

[4] Luke 14:26.
[5] Ann Stafford, *Angela of Foligno: Spirituality Through the Centuries*, ed. James Walsh, 1966.
[6] Evelyn Underhill, *A Franciscan Mystic of the Thirteenth Century*. British Society of Franciscan Studies, 1911.

his perpetual presence with her and promising to accomplish great things through her.

Returning to Foligno Angela lived a simple, frugal and semi-reclusive life with one servant-companion, 'a woman of marvellous simplicity and purity, and a virgin' to whom she confided her visions and in whose company she went out to the local leper hospital to minister to the sick and the poor.

Around Angela there gathered an enthusiastic group of disciples, her spiritual children, mostly men but some women, whom she instructed and counselled and to whom she wrote letters of encouragement and direction. Among her pupils was the talented young friar, Ubertino da Casale, a philosopher, preacher and leading member of the Spirituals, a wing of the Franciscan movement which advocated a strict and rigorous interpretation of the Rule as intended by its Founder. Ubertino's encounter with Angela was for him an event of profound significance, as he himself declares, 'When I had seen the splendour of her ardent virtue she changed the whole outlook of my mind. No one who knew me before could doubt that the spirit of Christ was begotten anew within me because of her.'[7]

As she advanced in the spiritual life Angela would proceed to the church of St Francis in Foligno, meet with her confessor Brother Arnaldo, and relate her visions and revelations to him while he faithfully took down everything she said, adding nothing of his own. He would then translate the visions into Latin, thus making them more widely known.

Angela continued in this manner of life, praying and delivering instruction to her disciples until shortly before Christmas 1308 when she became seriously ill. She died on 4 January 1309, in the Octave of the Feast of the Holy Innocents, aged sixty-one and was buried in the church of St Francis in Foligno. Although Angela was proclaimed a saint by the assent of the people she was never officially canonized, but was beatified by the Umbrian-born Pope Clement XI in 1701.

Her tomb was much frequented by her disciples and devotees, among them a member of the famous and influential Trinci family, a

---

[7] Arbor Vitae Crucifixae Jesus. Ubertino da Casale. Quoted in Evelyn Underhill *Mystics of the Church*, ch. 5. Cambridge, 1925/1975.

name one often encounters in Foligno today. He was Paul da Trinci, born in the year of Angela's death, and like her, a strong advocate of a rigorous adherence to Franciscan poverty and austerity. Dismayed by the laxity of his fellow friars, he established and led a small community in the wild and hilly region of Brugliano on the borders of Umbria and the Marches of Ancona, living a life of strict discipline and frugality. His movement spread until by the end of the century there were twenty such religious houses in the province of Umbria. By then Paul was old and blind and for the last few months of his life he lived in the Franciscan monastery in Foligno, constantly visiting the tomb of Angela for whom he had great reverence and admiration.[8]

ANGELA'S BOOK OF VISIONS AND TEACHINGS

Angela's book of visions and teachings dictated to Fr Arnaldo, was immediately recognised as an important work of Christian Spirituality. It enjoyed wide popularity in different parts of Europe and a hundred or so years after her death it was almost certainly being read to the English mystic, Margery Kempe of Lynn (c.1373–c.1439), who tells us that many works of English and continental devotional literature were read to her by her confessors and clergy friends. Margery's own treatise contains ideas and expressions which echo some of Angela's, suggesting that she was familiar with this earlier female mystic.[9]

With the advent of printing in the latter part of the fifteenth century a great number of books became available to scholars and literate layfolk. The first Latin printed edition of Angela's book appeared in about 1510, probably printed in Venice, and was again printed in Paris in 1598 under the title *B. Angelae De Fulginio Visionum Et Instructionum Liber*. The oldest Italian edition is dated 1536 and was among the earliest devotional works to appear in the vernacular in Italy.

The lasting importance of her book is evidenced by the copious references to it, and quotations from it, by later theologians and authors

---

[8] John Moorman, *A History of the Franciscan Order*, ch. 29. Oxford University Press.
[9] See *The Book of Margery Kempe*, translated by Barry Windeatt. Penguin, 1985.

of devotional manuals, particularly by sixteenth and seventeenth century authors in Belgium, France, Germany, Italy, Spain and England. Of special interest is the influence it exerted on the spiritual writer, Francis of Sales (1567–1622), bishop of Geneva in his two most famous works, *Treatise on the Love of God and Introduction to the Devout Life*. The English mystic Augustine Baker (1575–1641) refers to Angela's writings in his book *Holy Wisdom* and she appears too in the works of Bossuet, the French theologian and bishop of Meaux, and Francois Fenelon, Archbishop of Cambria and wise director of souls (1651–1751).[10]

The Latin version of her book is divided into two sections. The first, the Memorial, consists of an analysis of the steps which she took on the path of penitence and includes an account of her pilgrimage to Assisi and a description of her sufferings, temptations and visions. Of this first section Dr Moorman writes, 'It is here that we see the quality of her visions and the depth of her understanding. As soon as we begin to read her works we know that we are in the presence of one of the great mystics of the Church . . . there are signs here of intellectual vision and interpretation remarkable in one who had probably read very little.[11]

The second part of the book, the Instructions, contain the teachings which she delivered to her spiritual children, presented in the form of letters and discourses, together with some more visionary material. She deals here with such topics as the Eucharist, the Passion of Christ, prayer, love, the value of humility and the bearing of adversity.[12]

HER MYSTICISM

There is a marked intellectual quality about Angela's mysticism, her visions and revelations, bearing a similarity to the 'showings' of the English mystic, dame Julian of Norwich, in which heavenly mysteries are disclosed to her understanding. As with Julian, when Angela says 'I saw'

[10] Evelyn Underhill, British Society of Franciscan Studies.
[11] John Moorman, *A History of the Franciscan Order*, ch. 29.
[12] The Italian version of her book, which we are following here, is divided into three parts, and although the arrangement of the material differs in the two versions, the substance of the material is practically identical.

she means that she saw, not so much with her bodily eyes, though she may at times have done just this, but with her mind's eye, as when we say 'I see' meaning 'I understand'. Angela speaks highly of the gift of reason, and she herself brings to her mystical experiences an analytical mind, eager to comprehend and interpret those experiences and to convey to her pupils the truths she has learned, though she admits that some of the visions and divine revelations she has received are of such an exalted and ineffable nature that they far transcend human reason.

The various aspects of Angela's mysticism need to be seen against the religious background of the medieval Church, for like all the other Christian mystics, her mysticism and spirituality is deeply rooted in and nourished by the theology and doctrines of the Church. She meditates upon, and has visions associated with, the central teachings of Christianity: the Incarnation, the Trinity, Atonement and so on. She reflects on the divine–human nature of Christ and sees visions of the Virgin Mary and the child Jesus. She receives enlightenment on the Three Persons of the Trinity, and concentrates particularly on the doctrine of the Atonement and the sufferings of the Saviour. Consistent with the medieval emphasis on the sacraments of Penance and the Eucharist, she pays special attention to these particular sacraments, drawing from her own experience to instruct her pupils, and speaking of the Eucharist as a holy mystery, a sacrament of love and grace to those who receive it in the spirit of humility, repentance and faith.

Angela's progress in the spiritual life follows the traditional stages of the Mystic Way: the Way of Purgation, the Way of Illumination and the Way of Union. In Purgation the soul is awakened to its own sinfulness and imperfection and is stirred to repentance and confession. Thus purged, the soul reaches the second stage of Illumination and per-ceives the transcendent beauty and goodness of God, and from now on, God becomes the sole object of its quest; like the Psalmist it longs and thirsts for God.[13] In the final and most perfect stage of its spiritual journey, the Way of Union, God draws the soul to himself, enraptures it and unites it to himself in a loving embrace. These three stages through which the contemplative passes constitute a spiritual journey which is steep and arduous and fraught with many trials and

[13] Psalm 42:1-2.

temptations, but the reward is God himself, the end of man's striving, his ultimate and supreme joy.

We may single out a few of the dominant themes which occur in Angela's writings.

THE SOUL She speaks much of the soul, by which she means that invisible, intangible, immaterial and spiritual part of the human personality which can respond to God and which survives the death of the body. She says, for example, 'When the soul considers these things carefully and understands them, it inclines itself all the more to God'. In a remarkable passage she describes how the soul observes itself objectively and perceives with what great dignity and nobility it is invested and how greatly it is valued and loved by God.

GOD UNCREATE This phrase I have modernised to 'the uncreated God' which emphasises the distinction between the Creator and the creature, the Maker and what is made. God is self-existent, made by nothing and by no one. He is the sole Creator of all that exists. That which is made, is subordinate to the Maker. Therefore we who are made, owe our love and obedience to our Maker. Man, in himself, and of himself, is nothing, has no existence – a doctrine which flows from a belief in God as the Creator. 'Man's perfection' says Angela, 'consists in knowing God, and his own nothingness.'

THE BOOK OF LIFE Knowledge of the greatness and goodness of God is gained by studying the Book of Life, which is not, as we might suppose, the Holy Scriptures as such, but the life and teaching of Christ, the incarnate Word of God. We are to 'read' his life and meditate upon it. She reasons thus: Before human beings can love God and walk in his ways they must come to know him, and they can know him by studying and meditating upon the Book of Life and by constant and fervent prayer. The Book of Life is nothing else but Jesus Christ, the Son of God, whose life is an example to every human being who wishes to be saved.

THE PASSION OF CHRIST Meditation on the sufferings and death of Christ was a cardinal aspect of medieval piety and, as we would expect, figures conspicuously in Angela's spiritual life. Two years before his death

St Francis received the Stigmata, the marks on his hands, feet and side, corresponding to the marks left by the nails and spear on the body of Christ. This event was to have a profound effect on the medieval consciousness and to inspire members of the Franciscan Order to embrace suffering in the spirit of joyful surrender. Angela exhorts her disciples to meditate constantly on the pains and sorrows of Christ, and tells them that in doing so they would realise the costliness of their redemption and grow in love for the redeemer.

THE ATTRIBUTES OF GOD   In a series of visions which constitute some of the finest parts of her book, Angela is shown the attributes of God: his love, his goodness, his beauty, his wisdom, justice and power. In beholding these visions she appears at times to be transported to a wholly new level of consciousness and spiritual awareness, as are all the great saints and mystics. Bonaventura relates of St Francis that, 'Often he was rapt in such ecstasies of contemplation that he was carried out of himself, and while perceiving things beyond mortal sense, he knew nothing of what was happening in the outer world around him.'[14] The ineffable nature of Angela's visions leaves her amazed and utterly unable to find words to describe what she saw and felt.

THE PRIMACY OF LOVE   We shall not readily understand the medieval mystics and their ecstatic writings unless we first appreciate how wholly enamoured of God they were. Love for God and obedience to his will together constituted the driving passion of their lives and took precedence over everything else. Driven by such love there is little wonder that they employed the language of the troubadours in their efforts to describe the overwhelming nature of that love. Like a knight for his lady the mystics sigh and yearn, weep and languish, and are tormented and wounded by love. One glimpse of that transcendent beauty leaves the soul restless and craving for a fuller vision of God, whom they love and long for above all others. So we find St John of the Cross writing: 'End my torments here,/Since none but thou canst remedy my plight;/And to these eyes appear,/For thou art all their light.'[15] And

---

[14] St Bonaventura, *The Life of St Francis*, ch. 10.
[15] *The Poems of St John of the Cross*, II, tr. E. Allison Peers. London, 1947.

Angela writes: 'When I hear him named I am stirred with such devotion that I faint and am distressed for love of him, and anything less than God troubles me.'

RELIGIOUS AND LITERARY SOURCES

Angela's mysticism is, as we would expect, steeped in biblical imagery, her knowledge of the Passion narratives in the New Testament and the corresponding prophecies of the Suffering Servant in the old Testament, being particularly apparent. The influence of St Francis is everywhere present in her writings, with his stress on renunciation, poverty, penitence and humility. The various ascetic practices which Angela imposed upon herself have their counterpart in the life of St Francis, exhibiting her acquaintance with current Franciscan literature, especially Bonaventura's *Life of St Francis*. Powerful, however, as the influence of Francis was upon her, he was but a means of bringing her closer to Christ and of making Christ a reality to her, so we may say that Christ was her true spiritual hero, and that her mysticism was profoundly Christo-centric.

That aspect of her mysticism which is centred on the human Christ, God-made-man, and in particular his sufferings and death on the cross, vividly resembles the mysticism of St Bernard of Clairvaux (1090–1153), who, like Francis of Assisi, shows a profound attraction to the humanity of Christ. But that aspect of Angela's mysticism which centres on the transcendent Christ and the complete 'otherness' of God, who is knowable only through faith and love and not through human reason, is akin to the mystical theology of Dionysius and Areopagite. Dionysius, writing in about AD 500, was probably the Syrian monk who 'brought into Christianity a fresh and awe-struck sense of the unsearchable divine transcendence'.[16]

His works, written in Greek became known in the West when they were translated into Latin in the ninth century by John the Scot, and were to have a very great influence on all later Christian mystics. The beautiful

---

[16] Evelyn Underhill, *Mystics of the Church*, ch. 3.

vision in which Angela sees God in the 'Divine Darkness' is especially reminiscent of Dionysius's writings.

The poet and mystic Jacopone da Todi, Angela's contemporary and compatriot, living about fifteen miles west of Foligno, may have exerted an influence on her spiritual life. Echoes of Angela's thought and ideas can be recognised in some of Jacopone's Lauds, though we cannot be sure to what extent he influenced her or she him. Like Angela he was a champion of the original and austere interpretation of the Franciscan Rule and believed in a close imitation of St Francis' ascetic and frugal way of life. Like Angela, Jacopone was utterly hostile towards the adherents of the heretical movement of the Free Spirit, his hostility finding expression in several of his poems. Before describing the heresy of the Free Spirit it is necessary to say something about the essentially praiseworthy aspects of the movement from which it sprang, that is from the 'beguines'.

The earliest record of the beguines dates from the early thirteenth century at Liège in Belgium from where the movement spread to other areas of Belgium, and then to Germany, France, Italy, Spain, Poland and Hungary. The beguines were devout laywomen who lived together in communities, some in their own homes, vowing themselves to the keeping of a simple rule. Some of the beguines were married or widowed but many were single and while they remained so they vowed themselves to chastity, though they were free to marry if they wished. These women offered themselves to Christ, wore a plain grey habit, fed sparingly, attended Mass, received Communion, prayed, said the daily Office, and performed works of charity, caring for the sick and the poor. A characteristic and laudable aspect of their communal life was their custom of supporting themselves by various kinds of manual labour: spinning, weaving, carding and bleaching wool, making dresses, doing lacework, embroidering church vestments, and for the better educated and literate women, teaching, preaching and writing.[17]

It was from within this beguine movement that the heresy of the Free Spirit developed, though the majority of beguines lived virtuous lives and subscribed to orthodox beliefs. There were some beguines,

---

[17] See R. W. Southern, *Western Society and the Church in the Middle Ages*, ch. 7. London, 1979; and Fiona Bowie, *Beguine Spirituality*, pp. 11–42. SPCK, 1989.

however, who claimed that their oneness with God placed them outside and above the moral law and the institutional Church and its sacraments. They thought they could act as they pleased regardless of the discipline and ethical standards of the Church, and in the name of 'love' all kinds of immoral behaviour took place.

Wishing to purge the Church of the heresy of the Free Spirit the General Council of Vienne in 1312, denounced the beguiness, permanently forbade their way of life and excluded them from the Church of God. The Council, however, appreciated that some members of the beguine movement lived good and innocent lives consistent with the doctrines of the Church, and it therefore added to the stern denunciation a saving clause. 'We by no means intend to forbid any faithful women from living as the Lord shall inspire them, provided they wish to live a life of penance and to serve in humility, even if they have taken no vow of chastity, but live chastely together in their lodgings.'[18]

High-minded and blameless women sometimes came under suspicion, as did Marguerite Porete, the beguine who is now identified as the author of the spiritual treatise. *A Mirror For Simple Souls*, originally written in French.[19] In 1310 Porete was condemned as a heretic and burnt, together with all her writings, yet somehow her treatise survived and copies in French, Latin, Italian and English continued to circulate anonymously during the fourteenth and fifteenth centuries.[20] It was studied by many experts in mystical theology and was almost certainly known by Eckhart and by Ruysbroeck, in whose writings parallels with the Mirror can be discerned.

There are passages too in the writings of Angela which recall those of Marguerite Porete. Angela writes, 'Those people who know God best . . . know that all they can possibly say of him is nothing compared to what he truly is . . . All that has been said about God, either in speech or writing, from the time the world began, has in no way described the true nature of the Divine Being and his goodness' (ch. 38). We may compare this with Porete: 'Everything the soul has heard about God,

[18] Southern, *Western Society and the Church in the Middle Ages*, ch. 7. Penguin 1970.
[19] Marguerite Porete, *The Mirror of Simple Souls*. A Middle English Translation. Ed. Marilyn Doiron, OSF. Archivio Per La Storia Della Pieta.
[20] Margaret Wade Labarge, *Women in Medieval Life*, ch. 5. London, 1986.

and everything she may hear in the future, is nothing compared to the reality, which is beyond the power of the tongue to describe . . . nothing people say of him can be compared to what he is, and what he is cannot be said.'[21]

[21] Marguerite Porete, *A Mirror For Simple Souls*, pp. 69-71. Gill & Macmillan, 1981.

Part One
Visions and Revelations

CHAPTER ONE

Repentance Leading to Enlightenment

Angela summarises the stages by which she arrived at illumination of mind, beginning with repentance. She reflects on her sins and fears for her fate in the next life.

When I began to reflect on my sins, my soul was filled with such dread that I thought I would be condemned to hell and consequently I wept bitterly. I felt exceedingly ashamed of my sins, indeed so much so that shame held me back from making a full confession of them, and I continued to receive Holy Communion while still remaining in a state of sin. My conscience, however, troubled me day and night, and I prayed to St Francis to help me find a confessor who knew all about sins, and to whom I could make a full confession. That same night St Francis appeared to me and said, "Sister, if you had prayed to me earlier, your prayer would have been answered all the sooner, but what you have asked is already done."

The very next morning I went to the church of St Francis in Foligno and found a friar, the bishop's chaplain, preaching in the chapel of St Feliciano.[1] I decided there and then to make my confession to him as soon as his sermon was over. So I made a complete confession of my sins and was absolved of all of them, but in making this confession I felt no warmth of love, but only bitterness and shame. The next step I took was to perform the penance the priest had imposed upon me, and to

---

[1] The friar has been identified as Fr Arnaldo, Angela's uncle, who was to become her permanent confessor, spiritual director, secretary and scribe.

perform it with great diligence and perseverance. Yet I still felt full of misery and pain and deprived of any consolation.

It was at this stage that I began to be enlightened and to perceive that it was through the mercy of God that I had been given the grace to repent of my sins and to be saved from hell. I also wept and lamented more fervently than before because of my sins and undertook more severe penance. The fact that I could weep was some consolation, but a bitter one indeed.

I was now given such a profound knowledge of my transgressions that I saw that as well as offending my Creator I had offended those people whom God had created and given to me. Therefore I recalled all those sins I had committed and pondered deeply upon them. Then I pleaded with the saints and the Blessed Virgin Mary to intercede for me, and I prayed to the Lord, who had given me so many good things, that he would have pity on me. Knowing myself to be dead in sins, I asked God graciously to raise me to life again. Moreover I prayed that all the people whom I had offended would not accuse me before God. Then it seemed to me that all those people and all the saints did indeed have compassion on me, which stirred me to apply myself to prayer with greater zeal than before.

At this stage I was given a special grace to fix my eyes on the cross and to see Jesus Christ, who had died for me. I saw him as much with the eyes of my soul as with the eyes of my body, and seeing him there caused me immense grief, though I little understood at that time the meaning of what I saw and meditated upon. But I was given a greater perception of how Christ died for our sins, and this brought my own sins back to my mind so that I felt I myself had crucified the Lord.[2] Nevertheless I did not yet know what a great blessing the Lord's Passion was, nor did I understand at that time, as I understood later, how he had redeemed me from my iniquities and brought me to repentance and died for me.

As I gazed at the cross my heart burned so fervently with the fire of love and with remorse for my sins that, standing there before the cross, I forsook everything and offered myself to God. Although I feared very

[2] "There is the lamb of God, who takes away the sin of the world." John 1:29.
See also Isaiah 53:6 and Romans 4:25.

much to do so, I promised to observe perpetual chastity and not to sin with any part of my body. One by one I accused the different parts of my body of past sins and prayed to Christ that he would help me to keep my promise to live in chastity and to keep watch over my thoughts. On the one hand I feared greatly to make this promise, yet on the other, the fire of divine love compelled me to do so and I had no power to resist.

There was given to me then a desire to seek out the way of the cross, so that I might stand at its foot and find refuge there, where all sinners find refuge. I came to understand that if I desired to discover the way of the cross and to come to the cross, I must first forgive all those who had done me wrong. Then I must forsake all earthly things, all men and women, friends and relations and everything else, especially my possessions and indeed my very self.[3] I must give my heart entirely to Christ who had done such great good to me, and I must choose to walk on the thorny path, the path of tribulation. All this I must do, not only in my heart and in my affections, but in actual deed.

So then I began to give up the best garments and head-dresses I possessed and the daintiest kinds of food. At this stage it was a shameful thing for me to do, and very hard, since I did not feel much love for God and I was living with my husband at that time. It was bitter to me when people said and did things against me, yet I bore their hostility as patiently as I could.

By the will of God at that time my mother died; she was a great hindrance to me in following the way of God. My husband died also and shortly afterwards all my children.[4] Because I had set out to follow the way I have spoken of, I prayed that God might free me of them, and I was consoled when they died, although I was very grieved at their deaths. But because God had shown me his grace I imagined that now my heart and my will were united to his heart and his will.

I wished very earnestly to know from God what I could do to please him, and he, in his mercy, often appeared to me, both when I was awake and asleep. He appeared to me fastened to the cross and bade me gaze upon his wounds, and in a marvellous way he made me understand how he had suffered all this for me. When he had shown me, one by one, all

---

[3] Luke 14:26-27. Introduction. *The Life of Angela of Foligno.*
[4] Introduction. *Life.*

the pains he had endured for me, he said, "What can you do for me that will suffice?"[5] Whether awake or asleep I was always conscious of the great pain and grief he suffered. He showed me the pains he suffered in his head from the crown of thorns and when the hairs were plucked from his beard.[6] He counted over to me the scourgings he had received, and he said, "All this was for you."

Then all my sins came back clearly into my mind, so it seemed to me that I had crucified him afresh, which caused me great sorrow. Thus he showed me his Passion and said again, "What can you do for me that will suffice?" Then I wept and my tears were so hot that they burnt my flesh, and I had to wash in cold water so that my flesh might be cooled.

I felt moved to perform more rigorous penances, but when I reflected on what I was doing I realised that no penance could suffice while I was so attached to earthly things. So in order to come to the cross, as I had been inspired to do, I resolved to relinquish everything. This resolve was put into my mind in a most marvellous way by God, for I now began to cherish a strong desire to become poor.[7] My zeal for poverty became so great that I was afraid I might die before I had attained this state, and yet I was assailed by temptations against such a state. A voice whispered to me in my mind saying that I was young and that begging for money might lead me into great danger and bring shame upon me, and that I might be compelled to die of hunger, cold and nakedness. Furthermore all my friends tried to dissuade me from doing such a thing.

However, God in his divine goodness, illuminated my mind and gave me an absolute certainty about this matter so that I decided that even though I might be forced to die of hunger, cold and shame, I would by no means give up my intention to become poor so long as this was pleasing to God. Even if I were certain that these evils would come upon me, I would gladly choose to die for love of God rather than fail in my purpose. So now I was firm in my resolve.

As I persevered in my prayers I was granted a dream as I slept and

[5] I.e., "What can you do for me in comparison with what I have done for you?"
[6] She draws on the standard Old Testament texts foretelling Christ's sufferings. E.g. Isaiah 50:4-9 & ch. 53.
[7] In imitation of St Francis who declared poverty to be the foundation of his Order.

in that dream the heart of Christ was revealed to me and I was told that there was no falsehood in that heart, but only truth. He showed me too the wound in his side and he said to me, "Put your mouth to the wound in my side." Then it seemed to me that I did put it there and I drank the blood that flowed freshly from his side, and as I did so it was impressed upon me that by this blood I was made clean.[8]

Although I grieved when I thought about Christ's death on the cross, I was also consoled by it and prayed that my blood might be shed and poured out for love of him, as his blood had been shed for me. I desired too that, for love of him, all the parts of my body might suffer affliction and death, more vile and more bitter than his Passion. Then I looked for someone to put me to death so that I might suffer for my faith and for love of him. However I knew I was not worthy to suffer the kind of deaths that the martyrs had suffered, but I did truly wish that Christ would cause me to die a kind of death more vile and horrible, more slow and bitter than theirs. I could not think of a death as vile as I wished, nor one that would differ from the death of the saints, for I most certainly deemed myself unworthy to die the sort of deaths that they had died.

With these thoughts in mind I began to fix my attention on the virgin Mother of God and the apostle St John, and because of their sorrows, I appealed to them to obtain grace for me that I too might experience something of the pain of Christ's Passion. Then they did indeed obtain this grace for me, so that at one time I endured such acute pain that I have never since felt anything to compare with it. I perceived too at this time that the sufferings of Christ's mother and the beloved disciple when the Lord was crucified, were truly worse than any martyrdom.

Nothing now could deter me from giving away all my possessions to the poor, for I thought that if I kept anything for myself I would offend God who had so wonderfully enlightened me. But despite everything I did, my heart was still sunk in bitterness because of my sins and I cried out to God, "Lord, even if you condemn me to hell, I shall not cease to do penance. I have forsaken all things that I might serve you." Totally devoid of any sense of God's presence, it was then that I was transformed

---

[8] "The blood of Jesus Christ cleanses us from all sin", 1 John 1:1-7, i.e. his sacrificial death. A Eucharistic implication is clearly intended here.

from this wretched state in a most marvellous manner which I shall now describe.

I had gone into the church to pray and to ask for God's mercy, and while reciting the Lord's Prayer, God implanted that prayer in my heart, bestowing upon me a very clear understanding of the divine goodness and my own unworthiness. Each word of the Lord's Prayer was written on my heart and I spoke each word with penitence and sorrow for my sins. Although I wept bitterly because of my wrongdoing and unworthiness, nevertheless I was greatly consoled and felt something of the divine sweetness. It was in the Our Father that I perceived the divine goodness better than anywhere else; it was here that I best discovered it. But because in the Lord's Prayer my sins were forcibly brought home to me, I began to feel so profoundly ashamed of them, that I dare scarcely lift my eyes to heaven, nor to the crucifix, nor to anything else, but I commended myself to the Virgin Mary and prayed to her to plead for me that I might obtain mercy and forgiveness.

Then my mind was enlightened and I understood very clearly that I had indeed obtained grace and mercy and forgiveness, and that I had been given a faith that was more than merely human. Compared to the faith that I had now it seemed to me that the faith I previously had was lifeless, and so also were my tears. Consequently now I grieved more fervently over the Passion of Christ and the sufferings of his mother than ever before. Everything I did, however great or small, seemed to me of little account. I wished only to do greater penance and to enter more fully into Christ's Passion, for I had been given hope that by his Passion I might be saved. Moreover at this stage I began to find solace in dreams, and whether asleep or awake I felt the sweetness of God's presence in my heart. Yet my joy was still mingled with bitterness. I had no rest in my heart and wanted assurance and was always wanting God to show me more and more mercies.

At the last stage of my enlightenment I began to comprehend God more vividly and to experience visions and to hear him speaking to me. I took such delight in prayer that sometimes I forgot to eat. I wished that there need be no necessity to eat, so that I might always be at prayer, and indeed I was sometimes tempted not to eat, or to eat very little, but then I perceived that this was a snare which I must avoid. Yet there was such a fire of love in my heart that I never grew tired of being on my knees, or performing some penance or other. So intense was the fervour of my love for God that if I heard anyone speaking of him I cried aloud, and if anyone had been there with an axe, ready to kill me, I could not have refrained from crying aloud in this manner. This happened for the first time when I sold a small piece of land, the best possession I had, so that I could give the money to the poor.

I laughed at myself at first for behaving like this but then I perceived that I could in no way do otherwise. Subsequently it often happened that when God was spoken of I uttered great cries, even if I was in the company of others, no matter who they were. When people said I was out of my mind I replied that I was sick and could not help myself, for I was ashamed of the way I cried out like this. Also when I saw a picture of the Passion of Christ, I could scarcely control myself and was seized with a kind of fever and fell sick. Because of this my companion hid paintings of the Passion so that I might not see them. During these periods of crying, however, I was granted many visions, consolations and insights.

CHAPTER TWO

God Speaks to Angela on the Way to Assisi

Angela goes on pilgrimage to Assisi and during the journey has a sense of being filled with the Holy Spirit and longs to die. She returns to Foligno in great serenity of soul.

During the period of my conversion, especially after I had been so marvellously enlightened while reciting the Lord's Prayer, I experienced feelings of great comfort and sweetness and felt inspired to contemplate the union of Christ's divinity with his humanity. Such contemplation was accompanied by feelings of exceeding great delight, and because of this I stayed most of the day in my cell where I was praying, locked in and alone and utterly astonished, my heart wholly captivated by that joy, so much so that I became like a dumb person and lost my speech. When my companion came in to me she thought I was about to die, but I found her tiresome and a hindrance to me.

On another occasion before I had completed giving away all I possessed to the poor and having little left to give, I was saying my prayers one evening and feeling nothing of God at all. Lamenting this sense of God's absence I prayed to him in this manner: "Lord, what I am doing, I am doing only that I might find you; do you for your part, give me the grace that I might find you."

There were many other things like this which I said in my prayers, and then the Lord asked me, "What is it that you desire?" I answered him, "Lord, I do not wish for gold or silver. Indeed, if you were to offer me the whole world I would not accept it, since it is you, and you only, that I desire."

Then he answered me thus: "Strive diligently, and prepare yourself, for when you have accomplished what you are doing now, the whole Trinity will come down to abide in you and speak to you." Many other things like this he promised me which were a great solace to me and flooded me with heavenly sweetness, and from that time I waited for the fulfilment of these promises. I told my companion about these promises, yet with some trepidation, since these were wonderful things that had been promised me.

After this I went on pilgrimage to Assisi and to the church of St Francis, and it was on the way there that the promise that had been made to me was fulfilled. As I travelled towards Assisi I prayed to St Francis that he would plead with God for me that I might serve his Order well, for I had recently renewed my vows in regard to this Order.[1] I prayed also that St Francis would obtain grace for me to experience something of Christ's love and above all that I might become poor for his sake and end my days in poverty. I should explain that I had already made a pilgrimage to Rome to ask St Peter to obtain this gift of poverty for me, and by the merits of St Peter and St Francis, I felt that I had indeed received this gift.

Now when I arrived at that place between Spello and the narrow road which leads up to Assisi, and is beyond Spello these words were spoken to me in my mind, "I am the Holy Spirit and am come to you to bring you consolation, such as you have never experienced before. I will go with you until you reach St Francis' church, and I will dwell in you, though few of those who are with you will be able to discern it. I will accompany you and speak with you on the road; I will not cease to speak with you, and you will be unable to attend to anyone else but me, for I have bound you to myself and will not depart from you until you come for the second time to St Francis's church. Then I will leave you, so far as this present consolation is concerned, but in no other way will I ever leave you, if you will love me."[2]

[1] She had joined the Third Order of St Francis.
[2] Although on this occasion it is the Holy Spirit who addresses her we are not to think of the Three Persons of the Trinity as separate entities, for they speak and act in unison. What one says, the others say, and what one does, the others do.

Then he began to speak these words to me and to persuade me to love him: "My daughter, you are sweet to me, you are my temple, my delight. Love me, my beloved daughter! for I do greatly love you, and more than you love me." Very often he said to me: "My daughter, my sweet spouse, I love you better than any other in the valley of Spoleto, and because I have rested and reposed in you, do you also rest and repose in me!" Then he said that there are few people these days who are truly good and that there is little faith to be found, and then added, "The love of the soul who loves me without sin, is one who loves me perfectly, and I will show great mercy to that soul." Then he set before me the truth of his incarnation and his cross, and expounded to me his Passion, which he endured for mankind even though he was all-powerful and glorious. Then he said, "See now whether there is anything in me but love."

Then he said to me again, "My beloved daughter, you are sweet to me, see to it that you love me. The love which I bear to the soul who loves me without sin is boundless." Then I thought I understood that God wishes to be loved with that same love which he bears to the soul, according to the power and virtue of that soul. Again he said, "My beloved and my bride, love me! If only you will love me, then all your life, all you do, your eating and drinking and sleeping will be pleasing to me. I will accomplish great things through you for all the people to witness, and you will be known and glorified, and many shall praise my name because of you."

These and many other such things he said to me, and when I heard him speak to me like this, I counted over my sins and thought about my transgressions and how I was unworthy of such great love. Then I began to cast doubt on the words he had spoken to me and I said to him, "If you were truly the Holy Spirit you would not say such things to me, for I am weak and frail and in danger of becoming proud and vain because of these words." But he replied, "Reflect for a moment and see if you could become vainglorious because of what I say; think of other things and you will see the folly of such pride." Then I endeavoured to grow proud so that I might prove the truth of what he said, and I began to gaze upon the vineyards, so that I might learn the folly of my words. And everywhere I looked, he said to me, "Behold and see! this is my creation."[3] And at these words I felt the most ineffable joy and sweetness.

Then I was given a clear remembrance of my sins, and I saw nothing in myself but iniquities and offences, and as a consequence I felt deeply humbled. Then Jesus told me that I was loved, and that he, who was the Son of God and Son of Mary, had inclined himself to me and had come to speak with me. This is what he said to me, "If all the people of the world were to come to you now, you could not speak to any of them, for when I come to you, there comes more than the world. I am he who was crucified for you, and for your sake I endured hunger and thirst and shed my blood." Then he rehearsed his Passion to me and said, "Ask mercy for yourself and your companions and for whom you will, for I am much more ready to give than you are to receive . . . Go, now and attempt to speak with your companions; think of anything you will, good or evil, and you will see that you are not able to think of anything except me, for I am he who alone can bind the thoughts.[4] I do all these things for you, not because of your merits, but because of my goodness."

The people who had come with me on pilgrimage to Assisi perceived something of my languor, for at each word that was spoken to me by God the Holy Spirit, I experienced indescribable joy and sweetness. I had no desire to reach the city, nor did I wish that the road I was on would ever come to an end. I can never adequately describe the delight I felt, especially when God said to me, "I am the Holy Spirit who am entering into your soul." But I also sensed a feeling of great happiness at each of the things he said to me. This was the way in which I arrived at St Francis' church in Assisi, and as the Holy Spirit had foretold, he did not leave me, but remained with me, even when I sat down to eat, and he was with me until I came to St Francis' church for a second time.

When I entered the church for the second time I bent my knees and looked at a picture of St Francis reclining on Christ's breast. Then I heard Christ telling me, "I will hold you to myself like this, much closer than bodily eyes can see or comprehend. Now, beloved daughter, temple of my delight, the time has come when I must depart from you, as far as this consolation is concerned, but I will never leave you if you will continue to love me."

[3] I.e., she is taught that if God is the author and creator of all things, creaturely pride is but foolishness.

[4] When God speaks he compels our attention.

Though these words were bitter to me they were also full of joy. Then I looked that I might see with the eyes of my body as well as with the eyes of my mind and my soul, and I saw. But if you wish to know what I saw, truly I can only say that it was a thing of great majesty, beyond my power to describe. More than this I cannot say, except that it seemed to me to be full of all goodness. Then he departed from me, not suddenly, but slowly and gradually and with great gentleness. But when he had gone I fell down and began to cry out with a loud voice, clamouring and calling out unashamedly, "Why, oh Love, do you leave me in this manner? Before now I have never known you." More than this I could not speak, for my voice was suffocated with crying and I could hardly utter these words.[5]

This clamouring and crying came upon me when I entered the church of St Francis for the second time, and those who were with me and knew me, were ashamed of me and stood far away because they thought I behaved like this for some other reason. But the certainty remained with me that God had spoken with me, and because of his abundant goodness and because I felt grieved at his departure I cried aloud and wanted to die, the anguish of being separated from him being so strong that all my joints and limbs seemed to fall apart.

After this I left Assisi and went on my way, speaking of God and feeling much comfort in my soul. Only with great difficulty did I hold my peace and refrain from talking too much about God because of the people. Then Christ said to me, "I will give you a sign by which you may know that it is I who have spoken to you. This sign is my cross and the love of God which I will infuse into your soul and which will remain with you for ever. Then immediately I felt the cross and the love of God entering into my soul and spreading through my body. I actually felt it physically, and feeling it, my soul melted with love for God.

Blessed are you, Almighty God, the Father of our Lord Jesus Christ. You are the one who comforts us in our troubles, and have

---

[5] Compare with St Bernard's feeling of desolation at the seeming departure of Christ from his soul. "The feeling of chill, inertia and depression is to me the sign of his departure, and my soul is perforce cast down until he comes again and signals his return by rekindling as before the heart within my breast." Sermon on the Song of Songs (no. 74), Pauline Matarasso, *The Cistercian World*, Penguin 1993. See pp. 80–1.

deigned to comfort me, a sinner, in all my tribulations.

When I had returned home to Foligno I felt immensely peaceful and serene, beyond my power to describe, and because of this my life seemed tedious and I longed to die, that I might attain that heavenly joy, of which I had recently had a foretaste. This is why I yearned to depart from this world. Life was a greater sorrow to me than the deaths of my mother and children had been, more heavy than any sorrow I can think of.

For eight days I remained in the house feeling very weak and I cried, "Lord, have mercy on me and let me no longer remain in this world." After this I was aware of indescribable scents and fragrances, and these and other things filled me with such infinite joy and felicity that words fail me in attempting to describe them.[6] On numerous occasions too a voice spoke to me, but never at great length, nor with so much sweetness and deep meaning.

My companion was a person of marvellous simplicity and purity, and a virgin. A voice spoke to her and said, "The Holy Spirit is in this cell." Then she came in to see me and said, "Tell me what is troubling you. Three times I have been told to come to you." I replied that I was glad she had been told in this way to come to me. And from that time onwards I related many of these hidden, secret things to her.[7]

[6] Other mystics – Henry Suso, Bridget of Sweden, Margery Kempe – report their awareness of delectable fragrances, but some more practical spiritual writers speak disparagingly of such phenomena.

[7] Angela's companion and confidant is traditionally named Pasqualina.

CHAPTER THREE

She Sees God as Supreme Beauty

In this vision Angela perceives God as Supreme Beauty and Goodness and is reassured of his love for her and his will that she should always hunger after him and search for him.

On one occasion when I was at prayer, my spirit was exalted and I heard God speaking to me with many gracious words, full of love. Then I looked, and I saw God who spoke to me. But if you wish to know what I saw, I can tell you nothing, except that I saw a fullness and a clearness, and felt them so abundantly within me, that I can in no way describe what I saw, nor liken it to anything else. For what I saw was not physical or corporeal, but as though it were in heaven. I saw a beauty of such exceeding greatness that I can say nothing about it, except that I beheld the Supreme Beauty, which contains all Goodness within it. And all the saints were standing before this glorious majesty, praising it.

Then God said to me, "My beloved daughter, you are dear to me. All the saints in Paradise have a special love towards you, and so also does my mother, and they will bring you to me." The words that were spoken to me concerning his mother and the saints seemed to me but a small thing, because of the overwhelming joy I had in him. I took little notice of the angels and the saints, since all their beauty and goodness came from him and were in him. He was the whole and Supreme Good, together with all Beauty. So great was my joy at hearing his words that I paid no attention to any creature.[1]

---

[1] Dionysius and Areopagite writes, "All that is comes from the Beautiful and the Good, has its very existence in the Beautiful and the Good, and comes into being

Again he spoke to me and said, "The love which I bear towards you is beyond measure, though I do not reveal this to you. Indeed I even conceal it from you." Then I answered in my soul, "How is it that you have such love for me and find such joy in me, for I am a contemptible creature and have offended you all the days of my life?" To this he replied, "The love I have for you is so mighty that I no longer remember your sins, though my eyes see them, for I have much treasure stored in you."[2]

Then I felt such a true assurance in my soul that I did not doubt any longer. My soul felt and saw that the eyes of God were searching within it, and my soul had such joy in those eyes, that neither man nor saint from heaven could speak of it.

When he told me that he concealed the extent of his love from me because I was not able to bear it, I answered him in my soul, "If you are the Almighty and omnipotent God, give me the power to be able to bear it." He replied, "If I were to do as you ask, you would have all that you desire here on earth, and you would no longer hunger after me. Therefore I will not grant you what you ask, for it is my will that in this world you should hunger and long after me, and should always be eager to find me."

---

because of the Beautiful and the Good . . . As Holy Scripture says, 'From him and through him and for him all things exist' (Romans 11:36)." *The Divine Names*, ch. 4, tr. Robert Bolt. SPCK, 1920/1987.

[2] The New Covenant which God makes with Israel, as expounded by the prophet Jeremiah, states: "I will forgive their iniquity, and their sin will I remember no more." Jeremiah 31:34.

CHAPTER FOUR

God Reveals his Power and his Humility

Angela sees on the one hand the magnitude of God's power and on the other his profound humility in inclining himself to man and all created things. By his power he gives her grace to profit her own and future generations.

On one occasion I heard God saying to me in my mind and soul, "I who speak with you am the Divine Power, and it is my will that you be of benefit to all who see you, not only to those who are present now, but likewise to all who will think of you, remember you, and hear you spoken of in time to come. But you will bring the greatest benefit to those in whom I dwell most fully."

Then I rejoiced greatly in my soul, although I shrank from receiving such grace, and I said, "I do not desire you to bestow this grace upon me, for I fear it would be harmful to me and cause me to be proud and to glory in myself." But the Lord answered me, "Do not concern yourself with this, for you have nothing to do with my manner of working. All you have to do is to cherish this blessing and to serve it well and to render it again to him to whom it belongs." Then I understood that if this were observed my soul could not be troubled or perturbed, and the Lord said to me, "Your fear of vainglory is greatly pleasing to me."

After this I went into the church and while there, the Lord spoke to me most sweetly and graciously, and this consoled me very much. He addressed me thus: "My beloved daughter, no earthly creature can console you, for I alone can do so. It is my will to disclose my power to you." Immediately the eyes of my soul were opened and I beheld the plenitude of God, and in this plenitude I comprehended the whole world, both here and beyond the sea, and the abyss and everything else, and in this I saw nothing except the Divine Power. The manner in which I saw this gave me such an assurance and was so ineffable, that through an excess of marvelling my soul cried out, "The whole world is full of God." Because of this I perceived that the world is a small thing.[1] I saw more-over that the power of God was above and over all things and that the whole world was filled with his power.

Then he said to me, "I have shown you something of my power and might. Look now and see my humility!" And I was given an insight into the profound humility of God towards humanity and to all created things; and reflecting on his unutterable power and deep humility, my soul wondered greatly and esteemed itself to be nothing at all, for it saw nothing but pride in itself.

This made me consider that I was in every way unworthy to receive the Body of Christ in Holy Communion, and so I refrained from communicating. But after the vision of God's supreme power and his profound humility, he said to me, "My daughter, no one can attain this stage of seeing my power and my humility, unless he is inspired by special grace to do so."

When I was in the church the Body of Christ was being elevated in the Mass, he spoke to me again. "See my power which is now upon the altar. Yet I am also in you. Communicate, therefore, for I who am worthy will make you worthy." So I did receive the Body of Christ and my soul was filled with the most indescribable sweetness and joy.

[1] Cf. Julian of Norwich. "He showed me a little thing, the size of a hazelnut, on the palm of my hand . . . and I wondered 'What is this?' And the answer came, 'It is all that is made'." *Revelations of Divine Love*, trans. Clifton Wolters. Penguin Classics, 1966, 1st edn, ch. 5.

CHAPTER FIVE

She Meditates on Christ's Passion and is Consoled by a Vision of His Beauty

The mystics often speak of the beauty of Christ, drawing perhaps on the Psalmist's words, "Thou art fairer than the children of men. Grace is upon thy lips."[1] To Margery Kempe he is "the seemliest man that ever might be seen."[2] To Angela his beauty is a sign of his divinity.

At one time I was meditating on the great sufferings of our Lord Jesus Christ on the cross and thought especially of the nails which I had heard were of the sort that caused the flesh of the hands and feet to be driven into the wood. I wanted to see those little pieces of flesh that the nails had driven so violently into the wood. Then I felt so immensely grieved because of Christ's pain that I could not stand any longer on my feet and I sat on the ground. Then I beheld Christ inclining his head upon my arms which I had stretched out on the ground. He showed me his throat and his arms and at once my grief was transformed into joy, a joy so over-whelming and different from all other joys that I did not see or feel anything else. The beauty of that throat was something most wondeful and ineffable, and I perceived that his beauty proceeded from his divinity.

He did not show me anything else except that most comely throat, most gracious to behold, the beauty of which cannot be likened to

[1] Psalm 45:2.
[2] The Book of Margery Kempe, ed. S. B. Meech and H. E. Allen. Early English Text Society, No. 212, 1940/1982, ch. 85.

anything else or to any colour in the world, except that it seemed to me like the clearness of Christ's body, which I see sometimes at the elevation of the Host.

CHAPTER SIX

She Sees God as Supreme Wisdom

She speaks of the folly and presumption of wishing to know God's secret plans and workings.[1] He works in his own manner and in his own time.

A man once asked me to pray for him that God would disclose to him certain things which he wished to know. But I doubted whether I should do this, since I thought it would be an act of great folly and presumption to pray to God for such a thing. As I meditated upon this matter my mind was suddenly carried away to the first stage of contemplation and placed at a table which was without beginning and without end. It was not the table itself that I was placed there to see, but what was on the table. I saw there the ineffable fullness of God, but can relate nothing of it, except that I saw the plenitude of Divine Wisdom in which is all Goodness.

In this fullness I perceived that it is not lawful to look for, or to wish to know that which the Divine Wisdom is going to do, since this would be to forestall and to dishonour that Wisdom. When I encounter people therefore who wish to know the secrets that are hidden in the heart of God, I am sure that they err.[2]

From the time that I saw this vision I have been granted the power to understand and to judge people and things when I hear them spoken of. But I do not judge them in order to make use of that judgement, which is always a wrong thing to do. But I understand and judge with a

---

[1] Cf. the serpent's temptation and the sin of Eve. "God knows that, as soon as you eat it, your eyes will be opened and you will be like God himself." Genesis 3:5.
[2] Christ warns his followers against prying into God's secrets. Acts 1:7.

true judgement, which is without error and proceeds from the Divine Wisdom.[3]

I can say nothing more of this vision except that the word 'table' remains in my memory. I have said that at the first stage of contemplation I was placed at a table, but of the things I saw on that table I can say nothing more than I have already said.[4]

---

[3] To those who are God's friends he imparts a measure of his wisdom so that they are able to judge with the judgement of God.

[4] This is reminiscent of the imagery of the messianic banquet which figures prominently in the parables of Jesus, e.g. Luke 14:15-23. See also Psalms 23:5 and Proverbs 9:2.

CHAPTER SEVEN

Her Vision of the Virgin Mary

*The medieval church attached great importance to the Virgin Mary and
her critical role in the incarnation and atonement, for she humbly complied
to, and cooperated with, the purposes of God. "Be it unto me according
to thy word."[1] She figures prominently in sermons, religious treatises,
drama and ecclesiastical art, and forms an important theme for meditation and contemplation.*

I was once exalted in spirit, though I was not praying at the time. It was
after dinner when I had sat down to meditate, so I was not thinking of
the Virgin Mary just then. But suddenly my soul was uplifted to see her
in glory and when I beheld a woman of such nobility, dignity and glory
as she was, I was filled with a marvellous elation, and the sight of her
produced in me an immense happiness. She was making intercession for
the human race, and so powerful and splendid was her humanity,
majesty and virtue that she was wholly ineffable. Hence my indescribable joy.

As I gazed at this vision, our Lord Jesus Christ appeared in that place,
sitting beside her in his glorified humanity, and although I knew that his
flesh had been wounded and torn, and his body shamefully crucified, as
I looked at him now I did not in any way grieve. Indeed it is impossible
for me to describe the delight I experienced in seeing him there. My
speech utterly failed me and I thought I was about to die, and indeed it
was extremely distressing to me that I did not die, since I desired so much
to attain at once that unutterable thing I had witnessed.

[1] St Luke 1:38.

This vision continued for three days in succession. I was not hindered from eating, though I ate very little and my body was in a constant state of weakness so that I had to lie down, and I did not speak at all. Nothing else hindered me, but when I heard God spoken of I could not contain myself for my immense happiness.

CHAPTER EIGHT

Her Second Vision of the Blessed Virgin

This vision occurred on the Feast of Candlemas, or Purification Day (2 Feb), when candles were blessed and distributed to the people and carried in procession symbolising Christ, the light of the world, as enunciated by Simeon in the temple. Simeon took the child Jesus in his arms and said, "Now lettest thou thy servant depart in peace . . . for mine eyes have seen thy salvation, which thou hast prepared before all peoples, a light to lighten the Gentiles and the glory of thy people Israel."[1]

When I was in the church of the Brothers Minor (the Franciscans) in Foligno on the morning of the Feast of the Purification of the Blessed Virgin, God spoke to me in my mind and said, "This is the hour when the Virgin Mary came into the temple with her son." This stirred me with very great love, and my soul was exalted to witness our Lady entering the temple. With reverence my soul advanced to meet her, but because my soul feared to approach her, she reassured me and held out her son to me and said, "You who love my Son, take him!" and with these words she placed her Son in my arms.[2] As I looked upon him it seemed to me that his eyes were tightly closed as though he were asleep, and he was wrapped in swaddling clothes.

Our Lady was weary from her journey and sat down. She did so

---

[1] St Luke 2:29-32.
[2] Other medieval mystics were said to have been given the privilege of holding the Christ-Child. For example, St Francis, Friar Conrad, and Bl Henry Suso.

with such a beautiful, gracious and pleasing gesture, that for the delight my soul had in watching her, I was not able to observe the Lord, whom I held in my arms, but was compelled only to contemplate our Lady. Then I looked again at the child who seemed now all naked in my arms, and opening his eyes, he looked up at me. At the look of those eyes I instantly felt myself filled with so much love that I was altogether overwhelmed. From those eyes there issued forth such a splendour and fire of love and joy, that it was wholly beyond my power to speak about.

Suddenly, after that, there appeared to me a great and awesome majesty and I heard the words,"He who does not behold me small will not behold me great; I have come to you to offer myself to you in order that you may offer yourself to me." Then my soul, in a most marvellous and indescribable manner, did offer itself to the Lord. I offered myself entirely, and also my followers who were committed to walking in the way of perfection.[3] I made an oblation of myself in everything, holding nothing back whatsoever, either of my own possessions or theirs. Then my soul understood that God had very willingly accepted this oblation. I cannot say how great was the jubilation and delight I felt when I saw that God had accepted my offering, and with so much joy and graciousness.

[3] "I pray for those whom thou hast given me . . . keep them from the evil one . . . sanctify them in thy truth." John 17:9-17.

CHAPTER NINE

She Feels Christ Embracing
her Soul

In this vision Angela perceives that just as Christ was made man, yet remained one with God, so in our fleshly existence we can be united with God who made us.

I was gazing at Christ on the cross and looking at him with my bodily eyes, when suddenly my soul was kindled with such a fervent love that even the limbs of my body were affected. I saw and felt that Christ was embracing my soul with his arm, even the arm with which he was crucified. This caused me to rejoice with tremendous joy, greater than any I had hitherto known.

From this time onwards there remained with me a clear knowledge and enlightenment by which I perceived that in our flesh we are made one with God. This delight of the soul is beyond my power to describe, yet there remained with me a complete assurance and certainty that this enlightenment was from God, and similarly that the words and warnings I had heard within my mind were also from God. I marvelled that I could possibly have doubted this before.

Even now when I am rapt in this vision and the thought of that embrace, my soul is so filled with joy that I can feel no sadness at all at the remembrance of Christ's Passion, though I see the wounds in his hands. All my joy rests in Christ crucified, and sometimes it seems to my soul that in the close embrace that I have spoken of, my soul enters into the side of Christ.

The joy which my soul has in this illumination cannot possibly be described, for it is so overwhelming that sometimes I cannot stand upon my feet, but fall to the ground and lose my speech.[1]

[1] A common experience among the mystics, due to the profound emotions evoked by their mystical experiences, which extend even to their limbs, of which they lose control. Cf. Margery Kempe on Candlemas Day. "She was not able to hold her candle to the priest as other folk did, but wavered from side to side like a drunken woman . . . scarcely able to stand on her feet because of the fervour of love and devotion that God put into her soul." *The Book of Margery Kempe*, ch. 82.

CHAPTER TEN

She Sees the Supreme Justice of God

Angela considers the mystery of existence, of creation, sin and redemption, and asks why man's redemption could not have been achieved without suffering.

One day as I was praying I asked God why he had allowed so much suffering to be laid upon him by the death of his Son. "Surely" I said, "you could have created us with twice the amount of virtue we possess, and so you could have ordained it that we should be pleasing to you without these sufferings." Then it was given to me to understand that God did this in order that his goodness might be more clearly manifested to us. Also it was a way of working which was most appropriate to our needs. Yet this did not entirely satisfy me as regards my understanding of the matter, since I knew that God could most certainly have acted otherwise if it had been his will to do so.

On a later occasion I was exalted in spirit and perceived that the quest for this knowledge regarding God's manner of working, had no beginning and no end, and that when the soul found itself in this obscurity, it at once wished to turn back. But it was not able to turn back and neither was it able to advance. Being in a state of anxiety and uncertainty, I was then exalted yet higher in spirit and enlightened so that I might see the unutterable power of God, his will, his justice and his goodness. In these attributes I comprehended clearly, and beheld what I sought to know. So my soul was brought out of darkness, and I stood on my feet, even on the tip of my toes with such bodily agility and renewal of life, as I had never experienced before. Not only was I satisfied in regard to the question I had asked, but also in regard to all creatures and even the demons and the damned. But because this was a supernatural revelation I am completely unable to explain it in words, although I understood perfectly that God could have saved us in another manner, if he had wished. Nevertheless I could not see how God's power and his goodness could possibly have been manifested and set forth more plainly than in the way it was.

From that time onwards I felt myself so contented and secure that even if I had known for certain that I was to be damned, I would on no account have endeavoured and striven less to honour and worship God than I had done previously. So vividly had I understood his justice and the rightness of his judgements, that my soul was flooded with a profound peace, quietness and strength.

After I had seen the power of God, the will and the justice of God I was further exalted so I no longer saw the power and the will of God as before. But I saw something as fixed and stable as it is indescribable. I cannot say more than this, except what I have already said before, that it was all good. And although my soul did not see love, yet when it saw that indescribable 'thing', it was filled with unspeakable joy. My soul was taken out of the state it was in before and placed in this most ineffable state. I know not whether I was then in the body or out of the body, but it is sufficient to say that all the other visions seemed to me less great and less marvellous than this.[1] In this vision I was granted to see the destruction of sin and the assurance of virtue, and because of this, I now love all things, both good and evil, well made and evilly made, for I no longer despise those things that are evilly made.[2]

I was left in great peace, and reverence for heavenly judgements. So now when I say "By your judgements, deliver me, O Lord" I say it with as much joy as I say "By your cross and Passion deliver me, O Lord." The reason for this is that I cannot recognise the goodness of God more

---

[1] Angela's experience here is reminiscent of St Paul's when he was caught up into paradise. Her words echo his words. 2 Corinthians 12:1-5.
[2] Cf. Julian of Norwich. "There still remains a deed which the blessed Trinity will do at the last Day . . . This great deed, ordained by the Lord God from before time, and treasured and hid within his blessed heart, is known only to himself. By it he will make everything to turn out well. For just as the blessed Trinity made everything out of nothing, in the same way he shall make all that is wrong to turn out for the best." *Revelations of Divine Love*, ch. 32.

plainly in a saint or holy person than in one who is damned.[3] Although this profound truth was shown to me only once, it has never left my memory, nor has the joy of it ever departed from my mind. Even if all the other aspects of faith should fail me, this absolute certainty of the supremacy of God, his perfect justice and unerring judgements would remain.

[3] The idea here is that both good and evil come within the orbit of God's will, his justice and love, for all his ways are perfect and just.

CHAPTER ELEVEN

She Meditates on Christ's Passion

Angela meditates on Christ's sufferings and the enmity and malice of his persecutors and conspirators. Her meditations result in the bestowal of two spiritual gifts.

As I was meditating on Christ's Passion he appeared to me and showed me the great extent of his poverty, for he wished me to reflect earnestly upon it. I saw that he was poor as regards friends and kindred, and poor in himself in respect of his humanity and unable to help himself. I saw how in his Passion he knew the hearts of those wicked and obstinate men who had turned against him and contrived to destroy his name. He saw too their cunning and crafty tricks, their evil plans, their slander, rage and fury and the preparations they made to cruelly torment and afflict him.

On another occasion I thought about the many causes of his suffering, and I saw that he suffered because his soul was most holy and sinless and therefore he deserved no suffering at all, for he was innocent of any evil. He suffered too because of his love for us, though we were unworthy of his love, ungrateful and hostile towards him, and we despised and mocked him even when he was redeeming us by his death on the cross. His holy soul utterly abhorred and hated all sin, and he grieved over the sins of those who conspired against him and crucified him. He suffered when his disciples lost their faith, yet he had compassion on them, and he suffered pangs of grief for his unhappy mother. He was woefully assailed on every side and had no one to help and console him, and he endured anguish of soul and body because of the pain they inflicted on his most holy and chaste body.

Taken out of myself, I was transformed into the sufferings of the crucified Christ, and by the divine mercy I was given two spiritual gifts. First, my will was so constrained that I could desire nothing except what he allowed. Secondly he endued my soul with a disposition which is constant and unchanging. I now possess God in such fullness that I am no longer in that state of variableness that I used to be in. I walk in such perfect peace and serenity of mind and heart that I am content with everything.

CHAPTER TWELVE

A Second Meditation on Christ's Passion

In this meditation on Christ's suffering Angela is shown that his love for humanity was true and profound and that there was no deceit in him.

I meditated with grief on the death of God's Son and endeavoured to empty my mind of all other thoughts, so that my soul might be wholly absorbed in his Passion and death. Being wholly occupied with this endeavour to cast out from my mind all other business I heard the divine voice speaking to me in my soul, "My love for you was no deception." Then the eyes of my soul were instantly opened and I understood that the words I had heard were entirely true. I saw that everything that Christ had done for us was for the sake of the love he had for us. Consequently I perceived that it was true that his love for me had been no deception or jest. His love had been perfect and profound. I realised that my love for him was quite the opposite. I did not love him truly, but only dishonestly and deceitfully. This caused me intolerable grief and pain, and I cried out in my soul, "Lord, I have never loved you, except with deceit and pretence. I have served you with lies and never truly wished to draw near to you for fear I might have to suffer as you suffered."

Now when I perceived how sincerely he had loved me and had drawn near to me to such a degree that he became man I felt very great sorrow and anguish at my lack of love. Then he spoke to me again, "I know your soul more intimately than your soul knows itself. If anyone wishes to feel me in his mind, I will not withdraw myself from him; and whoever wishes to see me I will willingly show myself; and whoever wishes to speak with me I will joyfully converse with him."

These words stirred in me a desire never to feel, say or do anything which would offend God. This is what he wants and looks for in his sons and daughters, his chosen ones. He has called them that they might think and see and speak according to his will and that they might be watchful to do nothing contrary to it.

CHAPTER THIRTEEN

She Sees God even though Darkly

*Angela sees God in darkness, obscurity, nothingness, by the 'via nega-
tiva', which asserts the utter incomprehensibility of God. He is beyond
the power of human intellect to conceive.*

There was a time when my soul was uplifted to behold God with such
clarity that never before had I seen him so vividly. It was not love which
I saw; on the contrary I was left without love and seemed to lose what I
had before. But I saw him darkly, and this darkness was the greatest
blessing imaginable and unequal to anything the mind could conceive.[1]

My soul was given an assured faith, a firm and definite hope. I felt
so sure of God that all fear was dispelled and I can never again doubt that
I most certainly possess him. In this way my hope is made sure, and I see
him clearly, yet what I see cannot be expressed by words of the mouth,
nor can it be imagined in the heart.[2] In this darkness I see all Good, and
in seeing it, the soul cannot conceive that it will ever be separated from
the Good, nor the Good from the soul. The soul delights so unspeakably
in the Good, yet it cannot see anything which can be related in words.
It sees nothing, yet it sees all things, because it sees this Good darkly. The

---

[1] This vision, more than any other of Angela's, shows the influence of Dionysius
the Areopagite, who speaks of the utter transcendence of God, who is above
intellectual knowledge and perceived in darkness or "not knowing". See also *The
Cloud of Unknowing* for the influence of Dionysius.

[2] "The more we soar upwards the more our language becomes restricted . . .
plunging into the Darkness, which is above intellect, we find ourselves reduced
not merely to brevity of speech but to absolute dumbness." Dionysius, *Mystical
Theology*, tr. C. E. Rolt, ch. 3,

more that the Good is seen in darkness and in secrecy, the more sure it is, and the more excellent it is above all things. Doubtless all other things that can be seen or imagined are less than this, and even when the soul sees the divine wisdom, power and will of God – which I have seen most marvellously at other times – it is all less than this most certain Good. This is the whole and those other things are but part of the whole. And because it is seen darkly this Good, which is God, does not bring a smile to the lips, nor great fervour to the heart, nor emotion or distress to the body as it does at other times, for it is the soul which sees all this, and not the body. The body rests and sleeps and the tongue is silent and cannot speak.

All the indescribable kindnesses which God has shown to me and all the sweet words he has spoken to me, and the great good he has done me, are so much less than this which I have seen clearly through the darkness, that I put no hope or trust in them. Indeed if it were possible for all these things to be pronounced untrue, this would in no way diminish the hope that I have in this Good which I have seen in the darkness.

My body is wasted by infirmity and sickness, and the world with its bitterness and cruelty drives me out. Demons also afflict me with many troubles and torments, continually persecuting me and molesting me, so that I almost see them falling bodily around me. Yet despite all this, God draws me to himself with that Good which I have seen through the darkness. I do not doubt that it was in that darkness that I beheld the Holy Trinity. It seems to me that I am fixed in the middle of It. It draws me to Itself, more than anything I have beheld before, and is a greater blessing than anything I have received from God before. There is nothing that can be compared to it. All that I can say of this seems to me to be nothing compared to what it really is. I even feel as if I do wrong to speak of it at all, since that Good so greatly exceeds all that I can say, that my speech appears to blaspheme against it.

When I *see* that Good and am *in* that Good, I remember nothing of the humanity of Christ, of God, insofar as he was man, nor of anything else that has shape or form. Although I seem to see nothing, yet I see all things. However, when I am separated from that Good, then it is given to me to see Christ, and he draws me with such gentleness that sometimes he says, "Thou art I and I am Thou." I see those eyes, and that face which is so gracious and pleasing and which embraces and draws my soul to itself with infinite assurance, and that which proceeds from those eyes and from that face is nothing else but the Good of which I have spoken and which I saw darkly. And it is that Good in which I take so much delight and joy, that I can in no way speak of it. But from that time onwards there never has been a day or night when I have not constantly rejoiced in the humanity of Christ, for which cause I long to sing and to praise my God.

I praise you, O God, my joy. Upon your cross I have made my bed. Instead of a pillow I have found poverty, and instead of repose I have found grief and contempt. Upon this bed he was born and lived and died. Upon this bed I have laid me down to rest, for it is the bed on which I hope to die, and by which I hope to be saved. In this vision my soul is uplifted and consoled by my most sweet God, to whom be honour and glory for ever.

CHAPTER FOURTEEN

She is Told that her Revelations are No Deception

One frequently finds in the writings of the medieval mystics the expression of a desire to be assured that their visions and divine discourses are not a delusion and proceed, not from some evil spirit, but from God.

At the Feast of the Blessed Virgin Mary, a little time after my conversion, I prayed to the Virgin to plead with her Son to give me some assurance that the discourses he had held with me were no deception. A heavenly voice then spoke to me in my mind and promised me that my request would be granted and added further, "God has revealed himself to you and spoken to you and bestowed upon you an understanding of himself. See to it therefore that you neither speak nor listen to anything except that which is according to his will." I perceived that these things were said to me with much discretion and ripe wisdom. The divine discourses of which I have spoken left me with great joy and hope of obtaining what I had asked for. Moreover I was informed that everything I did would be done with his permission.

Accordingly my heart was exalted above all earthly things and wholly fixed upon God. Nothing that I did or said prevented my heart from being fastened on him, nor could I think, feel or see anything that was inconsistent with his will. When I had been engaged in prayer and wished to go and eat, I humbly asked God's permissiion and he replied, "Go and eat with the blessing of the Father, the Son and the Holy Spirit." In this way he gave me permission, sometimes at once and sometimes later. After this vision there remained with me an indescribable sweetness and very great happiness which I do not believe will ever fail me all the days of my life, and there remained with me no doubt at all, and I was assured of all that I had asked. I was fully satisfied and persuaded that I had not been deceived in the conversations Christ had held with me.

CHAPTER FIFTEEN

She Seeks a Sign from God

God assures Angela that he is pleased with her and her companion and impresses upon her to strive to give light to others. She asks for a sign that his revelations to her are genuine. He gives her the sign of perpetual and unfailing love.

On another occasion while I was at prayer, exceedingly pleasant words were spoken to me: "Daughter, you are far more dear to me than I am to you. You are the temple of my delight, the one in whom I love to dwell. The heart of the all-powerful God reposes in your heart."

These words were accompanied by a feeling of immense joy, radiating to all parts of my body, so that I at once prostrated myself. Furthermore it was told me, "The omnipotent God loves you more than any other woman in the city. He rejoices in you and your companion. Both of you must strive therefore to make your lives a light to illuminate others, especially to all who desire to be your followers and conform to your example. But to those who do not follow you, your lives shall be like a stern and harsh judgement."

I perceived in my soul that this harsh judgement would be pronounced against the learned, rather than against the simple lay folk, since the wise and learned despise these heavenly mysteries.[1] Yet I was told that so great was God's love for us that he was continually with us. I was told that his eyes are upon us, which made me think I saw those

---

[1] "I thank you, Father, Lord of heaven and earth, for hiding these things from the learned and wise, and revealing them to the simple." Matthew 11:25.

divine eyes with the eyes of my mind and I was transported with delight, more than I can express.

Although these words caused me immense gladness, yet when I remembered my sins, I realised that neither now nor at any other time had there been any good in me which might be pleasing to me. For this reason I began to have doubts regarding those things that had been spoken to me, and I implored him to give me a sign, some tangible sign, like putting a candle in my hand or a precious stone or something else, whereby I might know for certain, and be free of doubt, that the words that were spoken to me in my mind were from God. Then he answered me, "This sign which you seek would not free you from doubt, and indeed might deceive you. Therefore I will give you another and a better sign than the one you seek, a sign which will be with you for ever and one which you will feel in your soul. This sign shall be one of fervent love for me. This will be a sure and certain sign to you that I AM HE, for none but I can do this. This is a sign I will leave in your soul, a better sign than that which you ask of me. I will leave my love in you, so that for love of me, you will be strong to endure tribulation. If anyone speaks evil of you or does evil to you, you will be thankful and declare yourself unworthy of such mercy. This is a certain sign that the grace of God is in you, if you endure hostility with patience, and more still if you are thankful for it, for I myself humbly and patiently bore pain and sorrow for love of you."

Then I desired that for love of him my torments might be as terrible as those of the martyrs, and that the world might cry out against me with their insults and slander. Moreover I was very happy to pray for those who did me evil, for not only ought we to pray for our enemies,[2] but we ought to ask God to bestow upon them special graces. I knew in my soul that all the torment one could suffer was but a small thing compared to the blessings promised in eternal life.

God left this sign so firmly implanted in my soul, and with such a clear and bright light, that I considered I could endure any kind of martyrdom for love of him. By this love in our hearts we are led along the straight path of salvation. Whoever wishes to tread this path must keep his eyes fixed on the cross, both in times of joy and sorrow.

[2] Matthew 5:43-47.

57

CHAPTER SIXTEEN

God Teaches her the Value of Suffering

Angela is taught that those who respond to God's invitation give him great joy, and those who voluntarily bear suffering for his sake are especially close to him.[1]

I prayed to God to show me which of his sons he loved most. He replied by giving me this example: "Suppose that there was a man who invited many dear friends to a feast he had prepared with great care, and suppose many who had been invited refused to come. Would he not grieve for those who did not come, since he had prepared the feast at great cost to himself and laid on an abundance of food? And would he not receive those who did accept his invitation with great honour? And is there any doubt that among those he joyfully received there were some he most specially loved and whom he placed near to himself at the table, eating with them from the same dish and drinking with them from the same cup?"

Then I asked God what is the difference between those who refused and those who accepted the invitation. He replied, "I have invited all to eternal life and have made preparations for everyone. No one can excuse himself for not being asked, but of all that are invited few respond to my invitation and come or are given places at the table."[2] Then he gave me to understand that he himself is the table and the food as well.

[1] "Insomuch as ye are partakers of Christ's sufferings, rejoice . . . If ye are reproached for the name of Christ, blessed are ye." 1 Peter 4:13-14.
[2] Angela probably has the parable of the Great Supper in mind when many refuse the Lord's invitation. Luke 14:15-24.

I asked him then, by which way those who came, had come, and immediately he answered that they had come by the way of suffering and tribulation, such as those who were virgins, those who were chaste, those who were poor, those who were sick, those who were patient and those many others who endured tribulation. I understood the reasoning and explanation of all this and every word delighted me. Then it was disclosed to me that virginity, poverty, sickness, the loss of children and possessions and other earthly goods, and indeed all tribulations, were sent by God to his children for their own good, even though at the time they did not know this and could not understand it. For this reason they were greatly troubled at first, but afterwards like true children of God, they endured everything with patience and thanksgiving.

Although these children find their sufferings bitter, they recognise that they come from God's grace and mercy. And because of the love, grace, honour and spiritual value which accompanies them, they esteem them supremely sweet, and are not down-hearted by their troubles. On the contrary, the greater their tribulations, the happier they are and the closer they feel themselves to be to God. I can positively affirm that this is so, that God's children do feel the divine sweetness mingled with the persecutions and sufferings. I have experienced this countless times and could not adequately declare how sweet the joy was that I felt when I was troubled or reviled by my brothers, my friends and my family.

CHAPTER SEVENTEEN

Angela Counts over her Sins and Offences

Sin is very often connected with the appetites and senses and different parts of the body, and here, in her meditation, Angela examines her conscience in regard to each of these bodily parts — eyes, ears, mouth etc — and reckons on how she has fallen short in respect of each. She condemns herself, confesses her faults and is healed and forgiven. Christ then shows her how he has suffered in respect of each aspect of the body and made reparation for her sins and the sins of all humanity.

I reflected with grief and sorrow of heart on the sufferings of our Lord Jesus Christ and thought about the shamefulness of my sins, and how it was necessary for the Son of God to weep and offer prayers and intercession for our sins and to die on the cross that I might be reconciled to God and forgiven for my sins. I thought also of my ingratitude and my failure to do anything in return for such a great benefit Christ had bestowed on us. I was astonished at God's infinite goodness and mercy and my own great iniquity and folly, and as I reflected on these things it was revealed to me that we are liberated from our sins and from the punishments we have deserved, by the Passion of Christ. This was disclosed to me with such perfect clarity that I could scarcely restrain myself from crying out loud in the presence of all the people.

When Christ appeared to me he told me that because he had died on the cross for us, nobody could excuse himself if he was not saved, for in order to be saved all that was necessary was for a person to act in the same way as a sick man does with his doctor. If he wishes to regain health

ANGELAS COUNTS OVER HER SINS AND OFFENCES

he tells his doctor about his sickness and disposes himself to obey everything that the doctor tells him to do. Similarly it is necessary in the case of spiritual sickness to show our sins to the Physician of our souls and do whatever he commands us to do. I understood that the medicine which Christ gives us is his blood, which he freely bestows on us without any price. It costs nothing to the sick sinner except this: He must acknowledge his sin and pray for forgiveness. Then the Physician, Jesus Christ, will heal his sickness and make him whole.[1]

Then all my sins were laid bare before my soul and I perceived that each part of me had its own particular spiritual sickness and I prayed, "Oh Lord, Physician of eternal health, I am sick and no part of me is without sickness and defilement. And because you have consented to heal me if I reveal to you all my diseases and infirmities, I will show you all the sins of my limbs and organs, my body and my soul." Then I began to point out all my transgressions and I said, "Oh Lord, most merciful Physician, see my head and how often I have adorned it with emblems of pride. Look upon my wretched eyes, Oh Lord, full of envy and uncleanness."

In this manner I endeavoured to count and to lay bare all the sins of my body, and when our Lord Jesus Christ had patiently heard me, he gladly and joyfully answered that he had healed me in each of these respects, one after another. He took pity on my soul and said, "Do not fear my daughter, neither despair, for even though you were tainted with a thousand sicknesses, yet I would give you medicine by which you might be healed of all of them, if only you would apply that medicine to your heart and soul."

Then the crucified one showed me how he had made satisfaction, and done penance for all my sins. "For the diseases of your head which you have told me about, I have made satisfaction. You set yourself up in pride and vainglory, washing, combing, anointing, colouring and adorning your hair. But for these I have done penance, suffering grievous pains when thorns pierced my head, my hair was plucked out, my head was beaten with a rod, and I suffered all manner of mockery and scorn.

For the sins of your face which you have incurred by washing and anointing it and displaying it to men, seeking their favour, I have made

[1] "It is not the healthy who need a doctor, but the sick." Mark 2:17.

satisfaction. Wicked men spat in my face and made it filthy and soiled. It was swollen and deformed by rough and heavy blows.

For the sins of your eyes which have gazed at vain and harmful things, and delighted in things that are opposed to God, I have made satisfaction. I shed copious and bitter tears, I was blindfolded and my eyes were filled with blood.

For the ears that have offended God by listening to vain and evil things and taken delight in them, I have done great penance, hearing slanders, curses, false accusations, insults, mockings, lies, blasphemies and, at the last, the wicked judgement against me.

Because of the sins of your mouth and throat and the pleasure you took in feasting and drunkenness and delicate foods, my mouth was parched and empty, hungry and thirsty, and bitter with vinegar mingled with gall.[2]

For the sins of your tongue which you let loose in lies and slanders, blasphemies and derisions, I closed my mouth and uttered no word against my accusers and false witnesses.

For the sins of your hands and arms with which you have done much evil in embraces and touches and other iniquities, my arms were outstretched on the cross and my hands driven through with nails.

For the sins of your feet, vain running and dancing and loose walking about for pleasure, my feet were bound and twisted and nailed on the wood of the cross.

For the sins of your body, giving it up to pleasure, rest and idleness, my body was fastened to the cross, terribly beaten and stretched out like a skin, exposed to the wind and the air, gazed on and mocked by the people.

For the offences you committed with your wealth, acquiring it, gloating over it, hoarding it, spending it wrongfully, I have been poor, possessing no money, no house, no goods.

What more can I say? There is no sin or disease of the soul for which I have not purchased the true medicine. Do not grieve any longer. Suffer here with me, have pity on me always, be my companion in poverty and contempt."

[2] Cf. the Lauds of Jacopone da Todi, who writes on the dangers of the Five Senses. "Careful not to trip, my friend, take care./Shield your eyes from what you see./Close your ears to vanities./Keep watch over the joys of taste." Laud 6.

The crucified one spoke further to me: "When my children have departed from me through sin and have made themselves children of the devil, their return to the Father is met with great rejoicing. So great is the Father's joy at their return that he bestows upon them a supernatural grace, different from that which is given to virgins who have not departed from him through sin.[3] He does this because of his abundant love for them and because of his pity for their wretched condition, and also because they have sinned against so great a majesty. For these reasons even those who have been the greatest sinners may find the greatest grace and mercy."

---

[3] She seems to be thinking here of those who have sinned against chastity and who require a special grace to return to chastity and to remain on that path, a different grace from that required by virgins who may not have sinned in this respect.

CHAPTER EIGHTEEN

She and her Companion Visit and Serve the Sick

Although the medieval mystics occupied much of their time in prayer they did not neglect the practical side of religion. They visited and tended the sick and the poor and performed other charitable works.

At one time I was sick and was lying down feeling very weak when Jesus Christ, the consoler appeared to me. I perceived that he had great compassion on me and he said, "I am here to serve you." He stood by my bed in so gracious and pleasing a manner that I can in no way express the joy and supreme delight I felt. It was wholly ineffable, and I saw that this was the way he was serving me, by revealing himself to me in this manner.

On a certain Holy Thursday I said to my companion, "Let us go and look for Christ crucified among the poor and sick and suffering people at the hospital." So we took the scarves which we wore on our heads, not having anything else to give, and we gave them to the servant at the hospital and told her to sell them, and with the money to buy something for the poor people to eat. At first she was afraid to do this and said she would only be scorned, but because of our insistence she went and sold those little head-scarves and bought some fish with the money. To this we added the bread which had been given to us for our own sustenance.

After this we washed the feet of the poor women and the hands of the men, and especially those of one of the lepers which were all putrified and full of corruption.

CHAPTER NINETEEN

God is Everywhere, In and Over All Things

In these two visions Angela describes the experience of being taken over by God and illuminated by him, the soul being in a passive state, not expecting or seeking anything from him. She describes also the nobility of the human soul.

During the season of Lent my soul was exalted and I was made one with God in a manner I was not accustomed to. I felt myself to be in the midst of the Trinity in a manner higher and more powerful than before, and the blessings I received at that time excelled all others and filled me with indescribable joy and gladness. In him I understand and possess all truth that is in heaven, on earth and in hell, and in all creatures. I see God in everything and perceive how all created things are certainly in him. I see myself alone with God, wholly clean, wholly pure, wholly sanctified, wholly upright, wholly assured and in heaven with God, and when I am in this state I remember nothing else. But when I remain outside of this state I perceive myself to be full of sin, obedient to sin, unjust, unclean, totally false and earthly.

I did not come to this exalted state of myself, but I was led and drawn to it by God. Although I would not have known how to ask for it or desire it myself, I am continually in that state. My soul is often uplifted to God without my willing it and without my consent. When I am not hoping to receive anything from him or even thinking of him, my soul is suddenly exalted, taken over and dominated by him. In this state of exaltation I understand the whole world and believe myself to be, not on earth, but in heaven with God. This state is far more excellent than any other I have experienced, so clear, so ennobling, so satisfying, so enlarging that I have never felt any other state approaching it.[1]

Once at the Feast of the Purification of the Virgin Mary (Candlemas) I experienced that same ineffable manifestation of God, and while in that state, the soul beheld a representation of itself. It saw itself more noble, more exalted than it could possibly have imagined or understood. I could not believe that either my own soul or the souls of those who were in Paradise could be of such nobility. My soul on that occasion saw itself in such a way that it could not comprehend itself. I thought therefore that if the human soul, which is finite and circumscribed, could not understand itself, how much less could it comprehend its Creator, who is infinite and boundless.

Then my soul came before God with the utmost assurance and had no fear at all. It came into his presence with great joy, and with that joy there came a new and excellent delight, a delight so miraculously disclosed, so new and clear that my soul could never have imagined such a thing. At this meeting of my soul with God, the most high God spoke certain words to me which I do not wish to speak of or write about. When the soul returned to itself it discovered and retained within itself an awareness that it could endure every kind of suffering and torment for God's sake, and that whatever might be said or done, it could not from henceforth be separated from God.

I understood then that God is omnipresent and transcendent over all his works and present in every creature and everything that exists, as much in demons as in angels, in hell as in Paradise, in adultery and murder as in all good works, in all that exists, both beautiful and ugly. When I perceive this unity and omnipresence of God, I rejoice in God, no less when I see a bad angel or an evil deed than when I see a good angel or a virtuous deed.[2] He most often presents himself to my soul in this fashion, and this presentation brings with it enlightenment and

---

[1] All the great mystics avow that this lofty state of contemplation, in which the soul is taken over and inundated by God, cannot be self-induced, acquired or earned, but is a pure gift of God.

[2] It might seem from this that evil deeds are approved of as well as good deeds and

many other heavenly blessings. For example, when it becomes aware that God is present, it humbles itself profoundly and is troubled because of its sins.

God reveals himself in a second way, a special way and very different from the manner I have just spoken of. This second way produced immense delight and happiness in the soul, as does the first, but it is a different happiness and joy from the former. In this case he attracts and draws the soul in its entirety, and works many divine things in it and with greater power and grace, filling the soul with unutterable joy and illumination. This presentation of God is what the saints possess in eternal life.

When he comes in this manner to the soul, the mind is enlarged so that it is able to understand and know God, for he himself gives power to the mind so that it can comprehend what he wants to reveal to it.[3] To the soul that is drawn now out of the darkness there is given the utmost knowledge of God that, I believe, could be granted in this life. This knowledge is given with so much clarity, sweetness and certainty and is so profound that the human heart, left to itself, cannot attain to it. Nor can my heart return to the knowledge and understanding of it, or the imagining or anything regarding it, except only when the supreme God allows the soul to be exalted. Therefore it is not possible to say anything at all concerning it, or to find words with which to express it, nor can the imagination or understanding in any way reach it, so immeasurably does it exceed all things.

The Holy Scriptures are so far above us, that no one, not even the wisest person in the world, nor one who possesses all the knowledge that it is possible for a human person to possess, can fully and perfectly understand them. There is no one whose intelligence is not to some extent overcome by them. Often, however, when my soul is exalted to know the divine secrets I understand why the Scriptures were written,

---

demons approved of as well as angels. But this is not so. She is merely enunciating the belief that God is sovereign over all creation, good and evil. As God says to Bridget of Sweden, "Lucifer is my creature and the demons are subject to me." Revelations.

[3] When one is absorbed in prayer, God sometimes reveals mysteries to one, which are not perceivable by ordinary human reason.

what they affirm and what they deny, why some people derive no profit from them, why those who do not observe them are condemned and why those who do observe them are saved by them.[4]

<hr>

[4] St Bridget of Sweden (1303-73), in a vision, sees a book of marvellous brightness, each word of which "speaks of itself, as if a man should say, do this or that, and as the word was spoken it was done." Yet the Scriptures represent something beyond themselves. "The book you see signifies the Godhead in whom is eternal wisdom and justice, to which nothing may be added and nothing taken away. This is the book of life, which is not written like the Scriptures, for the Scriptures exist in time. At one time they did not exist, and later they did. But the Scripture of this book is eternal, for in the Godhead there is endless being. In him everything is comprehended without change or variance, present, past and to come." *The Revelations of St Birgitta*, ed. W. P. Cumming. EETS, No. 178, 1929.

CHAPTER TWENTY

She Sees God as Transcendent Love

In a highly mystical vision Angela sees the love of God as comprehending and transcending all other loves, and which, once one has tasted, leaves the soul athirst for more.

Once during Lent I was feeling exceedingly parched in spirit and lacking in devotion, and I prayed to God therefore to give me something of himself, since all goodness seemed to have dried up in me. Then my eyes were opened and I saw a vision of love advancing gently towards me, but I saw only the beginning and not the end. There seemed to me only a continuation and an eternity in what I saw, and I cannot describe with any clarity what I saw by likening it to anything else or to any colour on earth. But directly this love reached me I saw everything clearly, more with the eyes of the soul than with the eyes of the body.

This love advanced towards me in the likeness of a sickle, though there was no actual or measurable likeness to a sickle about it. When first it appeared to me, it did not give itself to me as fully as I expected, but part of it was withheld from me. This is why I say it appeared in the manner of a sickle.[1] Then I was filled with love and inestimable satiety, though this vision generated in me a great hunger, so that all my limbs

[1] Various interpretations may be given to the imagery of the sickle.

(1) In Western thought the sickle or crescent symbolises paradise.

(2) In biblical thought the sickle represents God's harvest and the judgement to come (Mark 4:29 and Revelation 14:16).

(3) A sickle suggests something partial, a section of a circle, a circle symbolising wholeness and perfection. Perhaps the latter is most appropriate to Angela's vision.

and organs seemed to be loosened and to fall apart, and my soul fainted because of the longing it had to attain that which was withheld from me. I did not speak to anyone, but my soul spoke within me, crying out and pleading with Love not to make my soul suffer like this and to go on living in this state, for my soul considered life to be death.

Then I called upon the Blessed Virgin and the apostles to come with me to the Most High and to implore him not to cause my soul to suffer this death, but to allow it to attain what it desired, that is, to the remainder of righteous Love. In this state of spiritual weakness I prayed also to St Francis and the Evangelists, since the love I felt drew me close to them.

I thought I saw two sides to myself as though a path had been made through me. On the one side I saw this Love and all goodness which came from God and not from myself. On the other side I saw myself all dried up where there was nothing good at all. I understood that the love I had, did not proceed from me, but that it came from God alone. All loves were united in him. Then he gave me a greater love and a more ardent love than before and I was drawn to this love. Thus there were two loves. There was the love which I have just spoken of, the one which came from God and was so mighty that I did not know of any greater or more powerful. Then there was an earthly love, and between these two loves there is a certain middle place of which I can say nothing, so profound is it and so full of joy and unspeakable delight.

Because of this I wish to hear nothing of Christ's Passion, nor to hear God named in my presence, because when I hear him named, I am stirred with such devotion, that I faint and am distressed for love of him, and anything less than God troubles me. In comparison with this, that is with God, I esteem as nothing all that is related in the Gospel, or in other places about the life of Christ, for in God himself I see much greater and more incomparable things.[2]

In this state therefore there can be no thought or sorrowful remembrance of Christ's Passion, nor any tears, even though as well as this transcendent love, I am aware of the inestimable worth of Christ's precious blood by which the world was redeemed. I marvel at how these

---

[2] This does not mean that she belittles Christ and his Passion. On the contrary it was through meditating on his cross that she came to God. But here she sees God as infinite love transcending all things.

two things can exist together. Nevertheless the Passion shows us the way we have to go, the path we have to tread, and teaches us what we have to do. Such a state is higher than always standing at the foot of Christ's cross and continually remembering it, though the soul must frequent both the one and the other state.

CHAPTER TWENTY-ONE

Visions Concerning the Eucharist

Angela's spirituality is deeply rooted in the Church, its doctrines, creeds, sacraments, feasts and festivals. Here she meditates on the mystery of Christ's presence in the Eucharist.

While Mass was being said on one occasion I was striving in my devotions to think about the humility of God and his supreme goodness in coming to us in the sacrament of the altar. Suddenly I was elevated in spirit and obtained a fresh and clear understanding of how God comes to us in the sacrament, and it was disclosed to me that, by virtue of his divine power, the body of Christ could be on every altar. This is something we cannot fully comprehend in this life, though he said to me, "The time is coming when you will understand."

Then I was enlightened further and discerned how Christ comes in the sacrament, accompanied by a glorious company (of angels), of great splendour, which caused me to marvel greatly. I wished to know who they were and was told that they were the Thrones.[1] They composed an exceedingly vast multitude and were of wonderful brightness, and if it were not known that God does things by measure, I would have considered that the company was without measure, innumerable, for what I saw could not be measured in length or breadth, but was wholly indescribable.

Another time I was in church hearing Mass, and at about the time of the elevation of the Body of Christ, when the congregation kneels in adoration, I was uplifted in spirit and the Virgin Mary appeared to me and said, "My daughter, you are sweet to me and my Son." Then she

[1] Thrones – the third order in the rank of angels. Collosians 1:16.

made me understand that after the consecration her Son was upon the altar, and she told me this as if she were telling me some new thing, and she told it with so much joy. Her words gave me so great pleasure and delight that no one could possibly relate what I felt, for the Blessed Virgin told me this with so much humility, and with new feeling and with the utmost sweetness. Then she said, "May you be blessed by my Son and by me. Strive with all diligence and earnestness to love my Son to the extent of your power, for you are greatly loved."

Then I felt that Christ was truly in my soul, and I came to know that there is nothing which causes the soul to feel so flooded with love and delight as to have Christ within. For this fire of love is of the very sweetest, and when it burns in my soul, I know that God is truly there, since nothing else can produce this effect.

This sacrament ought to be regarded with the greatest reverence and humility, for he who ordained it was none other than God himself, the supreme and uncreated one, incarnate in his Son. God, therefore, who is uncreated, invisible, omnipotent, is contained in the sacrament. It is he who does all things, who is merciful, just, creator of heaven and earth, of all things, visible and invisible, who is here in the sacrament.

In the sacrament there is a lesser thing joined to a greater thing. God incarnate is present, that is to say, divinity and humanity are united in one person. Sometimes in this earthly life the human soul receives greater delight from the lesser than from the greater thing, since it is more able to understand and receive the lesser, which it sees in the humanity of Christ, God incarnate. The human soul is a created thing and lives in the flesh with its bodily parts. Consequently the soul delights in the un-created God whom it sees in human form, that is in Jesus Christ who is both Creator and creature, Deity and humanity.

The soul sees in the sacrament the union of many things, and from the lesser, that is the humanity, it is led to the divinity, and similarly from the divinity to the humanity. The soul that meditates deeply and thought-fully on the sacrament, sees here the ineffable divinity in which all the treasures of wisdom and knowledge and incomparable riches are contained. Moreover it sees the precious soul of Jesus, the holy and perfect offering with all the virtues and gifts of the Holy Spirit. And it sees too the precious and sacred body of our Redeemer, and the blood by which we are saved and given new life.

CHAPTER TWENTY-TWO

The Poverty of Christ

Consistent with the teaching and example of St Francis regarding poverty, she speaks of the poverty of Christ and how he warns his followers of the danger of riches.

As I was meditating on the life of Christ he showed me his great poverty. I saw that he was poor as regards earthly things. He owned no house or place to live in, he possessed no land, nor vineyard, nor garden.[1] He had no money, no gold or silver, nor anything he could call his own.[2]

He was poor as regards family and friends and did not covet worldly attachments and familiarity with the great and powerful, with kings and rulers, scribes and pharisees and priests. He deigned to be born of a poor and humble mother and was brought up by a lowly carpenter, his supposed father.

Above all he was poor as regards power.[3] Although he was omnipotent and nothing was impossible to him, he humbled himself and lived on earth as a man, sharing our weaknesses and human miseries, enduring much weariness, journeyings, hunger, thirst, cold and heat, austerity and hardship. In his bitter Passion he gave power to the sharp thorns to pierce his sacred head and to wound him sorely. He allowed the scourges to

---

[1] "Foxes have their holes, the birds their roosts; but the Son of Man has nowhere to lay his head." Matthew 8:20.

[2] Women of means contributed to the expenses of Jesus and his disciples. Luke 8:3.

[3] She clearly has Philippians 2:5-11 in mind as she reflects on Christ's poverty. "The divine nature was his from the beginning . . ."

hurt him and the nails to pierce his tender flesh, to wound the hands that had wrought so much good, that had been laid upon blind eyes to give them sight and upon deaf ears to give them hearing. He allowed the cross to bear him and to be lifted up on high, his body scourged and pierced and bleeding.

He gave power to the soldiers who crucified him, to the Jews and Pilate to judge and accuse him, to revile and insult him and to put him to death. Yet all these things he could have prevented with a single word. With a command to his angels, an infinite number of the heavenly host would have come down and in an instant overthrown and destroyed them all.[4] Yet he withheld his power in order that he might save human beings and by the glory of his resurrection make them strong to resist wrong and to endure tribulation with patience.

Thus did the unconquerable Lord of all become a sufferer. The Creator of all became powerless. He made himself subject to Satan, to mortal creatures, to tribulation, injury, pain and all manner of grief and affliction. All this he did for our sake and for our salvation.

Christ not only became poor in all things himself, but he taught us the value of poverty, saying that the poor are blessed. He uttered warnings to the rich who put their trust in an abundance of earthly things.[5] Yet in these days poverty of spirit is repudiated by almost everyone. Even those who read about it in the Scriptures, who understand it, preach about it, applaud it, reject it themselves in will and deed, in action and intention. The world hates such poverty, though God loves it and approves of it, and chose it as a most blessed way of life for himself and his followers. We speak many words in praise of poverty, yet in actual deed and works we blaspheme against Christ's condition of poverty. Blessed is the person who is led to follow Christ's example and to choose poverty in this world. Woe to those who seek after an abundance of this world's goods and in the end are sent empty away.[6]

The Son of God was given to us for a pattern and an example, as a teacher and a master, so that we might learn to despise the glory of this

---

[4] "Do you suppose that I cannot appeal to my Father, who would at once send to my aid more than twelve legions of angels?" Matthew 26:53.

[5] "A man's life consists not in the abundance of the things he possesses." Luke 12:15.

[6] Magnificat. Luke 1:46-55.

world. He sought not his own glory but that of the Father. Though he had come down from heaven he humbled himself, making himself like a servant, washing his disciples' feet, rendering obedience to God, even to the point of death.

CHAPTER TWENTY-THREE

She Describes her Bitter Sufferings and Temptations

A Christian mystic of Angela's calibre could not reach such heights of spiritual perception and become the recipient of such remarkable visions and revelations without great cost to herself in terms of suffering and temptation. In this section of her narrative she describes some of the torments of mind, body and soul which she underwent during the course of her life.

Numerous temptations were sent to me, so that I should not think too highly of myself, nor be inflated with pride on account of the marvellous visions and revelations I had from God.[1] These temptations caused me great suffering of body and soul. Demons afflicted my body with countless torments. Indeed I think it is scarcely possible to write about all the sufferings and infirmities that troubled my body. There was not one part of my body which was not in some way severely afflicted, nor was I ever without pain, sickness and weariness. All the time I was so weak and feeble and full of pain that I had to lie down continually. All my limbs felt as if they had been beaten and evil spirits tormented me with numerous troubles. I was perpetually ill and my body swollen. It was difficult for me to move about because of the pain in my limbs, and I was not able to eat sufficient for my needs.

[1] Cf. St Paul: "To keep me from being unduly elated by the magnificence of such revelations, I was given a thorn in my flesh, a messenger of Satan sent to buffet me." 2 Corinthians 12:7.

The sufferings of my body were immense, but the sufferings of my soul were, beyond all comparison, more bitter and more numerous. I can only liken myself to a person who is hanged by the neck, with his hands tied behind his back, and his eyes blindfolded, who is left hanging there by a rope on the gallows with no one to help him and no one to rescue him from his trouble, yet he continues to live on in his agony and is unable to die.[2] Worse than this I do declare that demons tormented me even more cruelly by hanging my soul, so that all strength was taken away from it and it was completely overcome. And since I had no power to oppose the evil spirits, I grieved terribly. At times I was hardly able to weep because of my anger and the fearful suffering I endured. Even when I could weep I felt no relief. Often my rage was so great I could scarcely refrain from tearing and beating myself most dreadfully, which caused my head and all my limbs to swell. Then seeing how downcast my soul was, and all its virtue gone away, I was full of sorrow and I cried to my God.

After this I suffered further torment, for every vice reawakened in me. But although these vices were reawakened, they had no power to overcome my reason; nevertheless they caused me much distress. It was not only that I remembered the vices that had assailed me in the past, but many others which had not troubled me before now attacked me and inflamed me and caused me immense anguish. However, they had no lasting power over me and I was greatly consoled when they began to weaken and eventually leave me. I perceived that these temptations came from demons and that I had been delivered into their hands. Yet when I recalled how Christ was afflicted here on earth, and lived a life of poverty, I wished my own sufferings could be doubled.

At times too I was hurled by demons into the most terrible darkness of spirit, when it seemed that all hope of virtue and goodness were withdrawn from me. Then those vices that were inwardly dead in the soul revived outwardly in the body. They were both those that I had never experienced before and those that I had. They caused me such acute suffering that I felt compelled to put actual fire on my body so it might quench the burning of desire. And this I continued to do until my confessor stopped me.

[2] Francis de Sales, on the trials of the spiritual life, quotes this passage from Angela's revelations in his *Treatise on the Love of God,* bk. 9, ch. 2.

When I was in this darkness of spirit I thought I would rather have been burnt alive than endure such anguish. I cried aloud and called upon death to deliver me, wishing that it would come in any way, if only God would allow me to die. I said, "If it is your will to send me to hell, Lord, I beseech you not to delay, but do it at once. Make an end to my life and throw me into the depths of hell, since you have forsaken me."

A short time afterwards I understood that such vices do not exist in the soul, for I would never have consented to them. It is the body which suffers such violent attacks, and the grief and pain they cause is so terrible that if they were to continue long, the body would not be able to endure it. Moreover the soul too finds that all the strength has been taken away from it, and although it does not in any way consent to the vice, yet it has no power to resist. The soul, then, seeing that it acts against the will of God, loses all hope of being able to resist, and so is tormented by those vices.[3]

God allowed one vice to assail me which was of such strength that it exceeded all others. But a particular virtue was given me, with which I was able to oppose the vice, and by means of this virtue God showed me his power in delivering me. So even if I had not already possessed a firm faith, this one thing alone would have inspired me with an unerring faith and hope, which I could in no way doubt. Virtue increased in me and vice decreased, and I was upheld by that virtue, so that I could not consent to wrongdoing. Also by means of that virtue I was enlightened in mind and strengthened, so not all the people in the world, nor all the evil spirits, could have persuaded me to commit the smallest sin. The vice of which I speak was so powerful I am ashamed to speak about it. Indeed it was of such power that if the virtue had delayed in coming to my aid, neither shame nor suffering, nor anything else, would have been sufficient to hold me back from falling into sin again. I endured all these temptations for about two years or more.

Apart from this there was a continual conflict in my soul between humility and pride which troubled me exceedingly. The humility arose because I regarded myself as fallen from all goodness and devoid of all

[3] St Paul writes, "In my inmost self I delight in the law of God, but I perceive in my outward actions a different law, fighting against the law that my mind approves." Romans 7:22-23.

virtue and grace. I recognised that there was such an infinite number of sins in me that I couldn't believe God would ever wish me to belong to him. I perceived myself as having become the habitation of demons, to whom I owed something because I belonged to them and was their child. Similarly I thought I had wandered from the right way and from all truth, and that I was only worthy of the depths of hell. I must make it clear that this humility brought no comfort to my soul, nor any understanding of the divine goodness and truth. It was the humility which comes from dejection and brings with it innumerable evils. I was aware of a back-sliding of body and soul, and knew that I was surrounded by demons.

At that time God, in all his power and grace, was hidden from me, nor could I in any way recall him to my mind, because he would not allow it. Thus I perceived myself as condemned. Yet I could not believe that I was the cause of my own damnation, because I grieved and lamented that I had offended my Creator, more than anything else. For this reason I strove with all my powers against the demons, and tried to overcome the vices I have mentioned. However I found I was unable to do so, nor could I find any remedy or way in which I could escape or help myself, for I thought I had fallen so deeply into sin. Consequently I was often plunged deep into abject humility, in which I saw my sins and the abundance of my iniquities. I did not see any way that I could make my sins known to the people.

Then in order that I might make my sins and hypocrisy known to everyone, it entered into my head to go about through the cities and open places with meat and fish hanging round my neck and crying out to the people, "This is the woman, who is full of evil and deceit, the slave of every vice and iniquity, the one who did good deeds so as to gain honour among the people. It was I who planned to let those who were invited to my house know that I abstained from eating meat and fish, pretending to want no more than was necessary. Yet all the time I was full of greed, and gluttony and drunkenness.[4]

Also I made an outward show of being poor and caused many sheets and bed covers to be put down where I slept, but contrived to have them taken up in the morning, so that no one should see them. See how the

---

[4] These recollections belong to an earlier period of her spiritual life.

devil ruled my soul! Look at the wickedness of my heart! Listen to a daughter of hypocrisy and pride, a deceiver, an abomination to God and one who pretended to be a child of prayer! I was given over to pride and the devil. I feigned to have God in my soul and his peace in my room, whereas in reality I had the devil both in my soul and in my room. Know this all of you that I have studied all my life how I might become famous for my sanctity, but I tell you the truth that I have deceived many because of the sins of my heart and my secret hypocrisy. I have been the murderer of many souls and my own soul as well."

At times I thought I would put a rope round my neck, a very strong cord, and cause myself to be dragged through the city and open places and crying, "This is the woman, who all her life has dealt in falsehood rather than truth." So that everyone should say, "Look at the miracle God has worked in making this woman reveal her sins of her own accord, and in making them known whereas once they were hidden!"[5] Yet even this did not satisfy my soul, for I had fallen into such a desperate state, that the world has never seen the like before.

[5] St Francis had forced a Brother to tie a rope round his neck and drag him through the streets of Assisi for relaxing his rule of abstinence and austerity and allowing himself meat when he was sick. *Mirror of Perfection*, ch. 61.

CHAPTER TWENTY-FOUR

Consolations in her Sufferings

Angela demonstrates by her experience that God is especially near to those who suffer, and that suffering borne with humility and patience is for the soul's good.

At a time when I was suffering much spiritual distress and had no sense of God's presence and thought he had completely forsaken me, he had mercy on me and spoke to me in this manner: "Daughter, when you think you are forsaken, then you are loved most dearly and are very close to me. A father who greatly loves his child will moderate the amount of rich foods he gives him, and he will mingle his wine with water because he does not wish rich foods and wine to harm him, but only to do him good. So it is with God. He mingles the trials and temptations he sends to a soul with sweet consolations, and he preserves the soul in times of trial. If he did not do this, the soul would immerse itself in an excess of immoderate pleasures and enjoyments. Now you see why I say that the soul which seems most forsaken is most specially loved."

Then he gave me grace to confess my sins and to make my Communion, and while Mass was being said I considered myself full of sins and offences. I thought that the Communion I wished to receive would be like a judgement on me.[1] However I was soon restored to a better frame of mind and given grace to put my whole trust in Christ and his merits. It was as though I were dead yet believed truly that he would raise me to life again. With this faith I made my Communion and was

---

[1] "Whoever eats the bread and drinks the cup of the Lord unworthily shall be guilty of the body and blood of the Lord." 1 Corinthians 11:27.

granted a marvellous sense of peace, and I was made to understand that all the trials that had come to me were for my own good. This Communion produced in my soul a desire to give myself wholly to Christ, since he had given himself wholly to me. I longed to die for Christ, so much so that I rejoiced when trials and sorrows befell me.

God consoles all who are in trouble, indeed he is nearer to us in times of tribulation than in times of prosperity. May it please him to take away my sins, and through the merits of his Passion, grant me forgiveness. May he bless me and my companion and also the friar who has written these things for me. To the God of consolation be all honour and glory for ever.

CHAPTER TWENTY-FIVE

An Illumination of Mind Concerning Salvation

Angela is enlightened as to the seriousness of rejecting revelations of truth and opportunities of salvation that are given to one. She likens this to a son who is given an excellent education but despises it and makes no use of it.

Once when I was praying in my private room the following words were spoken to me: "All those who are enlightened by God and instructed in his ways, but in spite of the light and revelation given to them, shut their ears so that they may not hear, and their eyes that they may not see, and refuse to heed what God has to say to them, all these, I declare, merit the wrath of God. They are more bent on lowering themselves to follow other doctrines than to follow the ways of God. They wish, against their consciences, to remain on the broad highway."[1]

Not only once was this judgement told me, but many times. I was filled with horror when I heard it, for it seemed to me a very grave matter and one in which there was no deceit. He spoke true words and truly denounced those to whom he had given his light and his grace, and who had despised it and fallen away. Then I was given an illustration and commanded to have it written down.

"There was a father who sent his son to a school and spent large sums of money on him, clothing him respectably in fine raiment and

---

[1] "Wide is the gate and broad the road that leads to destruction, and many enter that way. Narrow is the gate, and constricted the road that leads to life and those who find it are few." Matthew 7:13.

providing him with books and all things necessary. Then after the son had been taught, he removed him to a better school to advance him higher and to enable him to make more progress. But this son then behaved negligently and did not care about the knowledge he had acquired, but returned to his rough ways and vile occupations, soon forgetting all that he had learnt. Do you not think that his father would feel very distressed and indignant at his son's behaviour? That son would resemble one who had been taught the Scriptures and given instructions in sermons, and then afterwards enlightened and inspired by God himself, so that he might know how to govern his life and be an example to others. But suppose such a person should despise the light and inspiration and instruction he had received and sink into negligent ways, growing fat and debasing himself by ill behaviour, would he not merit God's displeasure and forfeit that light and grace that had been given to him? How pleasing to God are those who, not only read the Scriptures, but those who obey and fulfil them and follow the ways of Christ."

I prayed, "Oh God, you are my Father, you are my God. Teach me what you would have me to do. Instruct me in what is pleasing to you, for I am ready to obey you." Reflecting on these words all the morning I saw and heard, but am in no way able to utter what I saw and heard, but it was a most unspeakable abyss, and I was shown what it was and who dwelt there and who did not. Then God said, "Truly, there is no other straight way except that which follows in my footsteps. Upon this road no one is deceived." This was enforced upon me many times, and with great truth and clarity.

CHAPTER TWENTY-SIX

A Vision Concerning her Disciples

She sees a vision of Christ embracing each one of her spiritual children and exhorting them to discover the way of the cross.

At a certain time I was uplifted in spirit and absorbed into the Uncreated Light and saw that which cannot be told. While I remained in that state there appeared to me the image of God made man, Christ crucified, as though at that very moment he had been lifted down from the cross. His blood issued from his wounds, as fresh and red, as it must have been at the time he was crucified, and in all his joints there appeared such a disintegration of the sinews, caused by the cruel stretching on the cross, that all the bones seemed to be loosened and out of joint.

At this sight I was pierced with anguish to the depths of my being and was more saddened than I had ever been before. But as I stood there plunged in grief there suddenly appeared around the crucified Christ a multitude of my disciples, devout people, who had devoted themselves to preaching and to imitating Christ in his poverty, contempt and suffering. He embraced each one and made each to kiss the wound in his side. And because of the joy I felt in my soul at this sight, I forgot the sorrow I had previously felt. The state of my spiritual children, however, differed one from another, and our Lord pressed some less and some more into his side. I then understood in my soul that, in the same way as my children had been pressed into our Lord's side, according to their different states, so also to each one differently he spoke the words: "Discover the way of the cross, the way of suffering and contempt. I have chosen you that, through your preaching and example, my truth may be manifest in the world." In no way is it possible to describe the exceedingly great love which shone from that face and from those eyes.

I saw many other things concerning myself and my followers, all of which I cannot describe. But I will say this, that I have seen and understood very clearly that the blessed God does most tenderly overshadow us.

Part Two

Teachings

CHAPTER TWENTY-SEVEN

When God Lives in the Soul He Enlightens It

Angela teaches her followers how God reveals truth and mysteries to the soul which are above human reason. She teaches them that in order to find God one must fix one's mind wholeheartedly on him, avoiding all distractions.

My children, when the soul is united with God and God with the soul, then the soul is elevated above itself and illuminated and hears what God wishes to teach it. Then it rests in the divine goodness, of which no one can speak, because the divine goodness is above all kinds of words and of speech and of all human intelligence. But with great joy the soul, as it were, swims in the divine goodness and is enlightened and understands the meaning of all the difficult and obscure sayings of Christ. Similarly it comprehends how and why such great suffering existed in the soul of Christ. When I am wholly absorbed in contemplating Christ's Passion, I too experience great suffering and the thought of how his soul suffered brings no joy. This does not happen when I contemplate the sufferings of his body, for then the grief is followed by joy.[1]

God often works in the soul in a most marvellous way which no one but he can do, for he suddenly exalts the soul to himself with such rapture, that if it were to continue in that state, I do not think the body

---

[1] I.e., because the suffering and death of Jesus' body was followed by resurrection. The suffering of Christ in his mind and soul is so much beyond our comprehension that we tend to focus on the sufferings of his body.

would be able to bear it. And if the soul desires to hold fast to God, he instantly departs, although great joy and assurance remain, indeed such profound joy that the soul cannot in any way doubt that God dwells within it. These revelations and delights of the soul do not always occur in the same manner, but in various ways and almost always accompanied by something new. Yet none of them can be described, since the visions and revelations are at one time like this and another time like that, and so also is the soul's joy and happiness.

Of all this I can say no more. Truly if I were to speak of the visions, it would be to speak ill of them, to spoil them, to portray them imperfectly, yes even to denigrate them, rather than to show them forth as I ought to do. This is because of my own unworthiness, blindness and darkness of spirit. So I warn you my sons, be careful of what I say and only believe those sayings of mine which resemble the sayings of Jesus Christ, and which lead you to an imitation of him.

For the present, my sons, I do not take any pleasure in writing, for I continually bewail my sins and the Passion of Christ, by which my sins are forgiven. Yet I am constrained to write to you because of the letters you send me. Let me make it plain to you, my sons, only one thing is necessary to us, and that is God. In order to find God it is necessary to fix our minds wholly upon him, and we may more readily do this by giving up all bad and unprofitable habits and all unnecessary familiarity with men and women of various kinds, all useless knowledge and curiosity over new things; in short, everything which distracts the mind and leads one away from God.

Finally, we must reflect on our past actions, on what we are doing now and intend to do in the future, and how our fate in the next world will be determined by what we deserve. Then death will come, and it lasts for all eternity, so no day or night should pass without our considering these matters.

CHAPTER TWENTY-EIGHT

The Importance of Knowing God and Knowing Oneself

Knowledge of God and knowledge of the self constitute an important element in Angela's mysticism. God is known most perfectly through his Son, Jesus Christ, his life, teaching, death and resurrection. Man must also seek to know himself: his essential nobility as a child of God, his fallen nature and sin, his nothingness apart from God and his redemption by Christ.

There is nothing in the whole world which I delight to write about or to speak about more than the knowledge of God and the knowledge of ourselves.[1] My beloved sons, every revelation, all sweetness and emotion, all knowedge and contemplation avail nothing unless a person knows God and himself. Without this knowledge everything else will be of little profit. I am surprised therefore that you want to receive letters from me, for I do not see in what way my words can bring comfort to you, since I write of nothing else except this knowledge of which I speak, and I take no pleasure in writing of other matters. Indeed I have imposed silence upon myself in regard to other matters.

The kingdom of heaven is what we strive for, and for this, a knowledge of God and his son, Jesus Christ, his life and works, is necessary, for he has shown us the way. Before everything else it is necessary to know Christ and how he was crucified for us. It is particularly through his suffering and death that he has exhibited his

---

[1] St Augustine prayed, "O Lord, that I might know thee and myself." St Francis asked, "O God, who art thou, and who am I?"

infinite love for us. This benefit exceeds all other benefits he has conferred upon us. It is right that we should lament the Passion of our beloved Lord, and show our gratitude to him by transforming ourselves into his likeness, and by loving him as he has loved us, and by loving our neighbours.

When we consider how much God has done for us, especially in procuring our salvation in Christ, we are induced to contemplate our human condition, which is most noble and much loved by God, our creator. Indeed he loved us so much that he was willing to die for us. This he would not have done if man had not been a most noble creature and of great worth. Furthermore a consideration of Christ, who was crucified for us, imposes upon us a duty to work out our own salvation, since God, who is so much higher than we are, was so diligent to obtain our redemption.[2] So we for our part must look to ourselves and to our salvation by being sorry for our sins and so furthering the will of God.

The more we know of Christ crucified, the more perfectly do we love him, and become one with him, and share in his sufferings. All this is accomplished through our knowledge of God and our knowledge of ourselves and our own wretchedness. On the one hand we see the infinite nature of God's majesty, and on the other the vileness and unworthiness of sinners. But God himself has deigned to become the friend and brother of sinners through his Son, Jesus Christ. So the more the soul knows Jesus, sees him and meditates on him, the more it enters into his love and is transformed by him.

When the individual soul is illuminated by the divine light and recognises that it has itself been the cause of Christ's great suffering, the soul is overwhelmed by grief. This grief is multiplied when the soul considers that God, in his infinite goodness, and for the sake of such a vile creature as itself, humbled himself and became a mortal man and was tormented with immeasurable pain. In order to raise us up from our wretchedness and spiritual poverty, the most high God, Jesus Christ, who is rich in all things, made himself poor for our sake. He, who is most beautiful and most joyful, made himself wretched, in order that,

---

[2] "You must work out your own salvation in fear and trembling." Philippians 2:12.

through his suffering, he might redeem us and save us from everlasting damnation. The God of glory, who is worthy to be praised above all others, made himself humble and obedient to death, so that man might be made glorious and honourable.[3]

---

[3] "He humbled himself and was obedient, even to the point of death." Philippians 2:5-9.

CHAPTER TWENTY-NINE

On Knowing God as He Truly Is

Angela exhorts her disciple to strive to know God as he truly is, which will lead to loving him and desiring to be like him.

My dearest son, first and foremost it is necessary to know God as he truly is. I do not mean just outwardly and superficially, such as when we gain knowledge of something by the sound of words, by the colour of writing or by likeness to something else. I mean rather that we must strive to know him as he truly is, his supreme beauty, goodness, majesty, generosity, mercy and pity. He is understood by a wise and discerning person more than by a simple person, for the wise person understands him as he really is, but the simple and undiscerning person only as he appears to be.

We may give an analogy to make this clear. Suppose a precious stone had been found, which the wise and the simple person wished, for different reasons, to possess. The simple person will wish to possess it, only because it is heavy and bright, and not because he knows its true worth. But the wise person will want to possess it, not only for its splendour and brightness, but because he perceives its true value and merit. When the wise person has found it he will love it fervently and appreciate its intrinsic worth.

Similarly the wise soul will endeavour to know God, not superficially or by careless reflection, but by using all his powers, and making every effort to know him as he truly is, savouring his supreme goodness and knowing his priceless worth. For not only is God good, but he is Supreme Good. When human beings know him, they love him because of his Supreme Goodness, and loving him they want to possess him, and he gives himself to the soul, and the soul tastes his sweetness and enjoys the greatest of all pleasures.

Then the soul participates in the Supreme Good, and being enamoured of the Beloved, who is God, the soul desires to hold him fast, and embraces him, and unites itself to God with the sweetest love. Then the lover is transformed into the Beloved, and the Beloved into the lover, by virtue of the love that flows between them. Just as when hard iron is put into the fire, it assumes the colour, heat, substance and form of the fire, so that it almost turns into fire itself, so also does the soul, when it is united with God.[1] Through grace, it almost becomes divine itself, though it does not change its own substance. But its whole life is transformed in the love of God, and in this manner it almost becomes divine.

---

[1] She probably has St Bernard in mind. "As a drop of water seems to disappear completely in a big quantity of wine, even assuming the wine's taste and colour; just as red, molten iron becomes so much like fire it seems to lose its primary state . . . so it is necessary for the saints that all human feelings melt in a mysterious way and flow into the will of God." *On Loving God*, Treatises II, Bernard of Clairvaux. tr. Robert Walton, OSB. Cistercian Publications. Michigan, 1980.

CHAPTER THIRTY

Knowledge of God is a Gift of Grace

Angela explains that knowledge of God cannot be acquired by human effort alone. It is a gift of divine grace, resulting from constant and fervent prayer, and meditation on the life of Christ, which she calls "The Book of Life."

You must understand, my dear children, that the soul cannot find God and know him by any power of its own, neither by the study of books, nor by learning, nor by any created thing, although of course it may use these means and benefit from them, but it can only obtain this knowledge of God by the light of divine grace. I believe that the soul cannot find God more quickly and easily than by devout, humble, fervent and continual prayer. But prayer must not only be uttered with the mouth, but also with the mind and heart and all the strength of the soul and feelings of the body, making its petitions to God with ardent desire. It must read and study and meditate continually on the Book of Life, that is on the whole life of Christ, as he lived on earth.

God the Father, my beloved children, has set before us the way by which we may obtain a knowledge of himself. He has given us his beloved son as a sign to guide us and an example to follow. If you are eager, therefore, to be enlightened by divine grace, if you want to be free of all worldly cares, if you want to be free of all harmful temptations, and if you wish to perfect yourselves according to the ways of God, then be quick to resort to the cross of Christ. Truly there is no other way by which we may find God, and having found him, keep him. This requires continual prayer, for prayer illuminates the soul and exalts it and transforms it. Then it sees clearly the way that is prepared for it and which has already been trod by Christ. Being uplifted in this way our hearts are kindled with the fire of divine love and made one with God. Run swiftly then, my dearest children, to the cross of Christ, and pray to him who died for your sake, that he will enlighten you, so that you may know both him and yourself. May you have a profound awareness of your faults, rise from a love of sin to the divine mercy and cast away all falsehood and deceit.

If you wish to be enlightened and well instructed read the Book of Life, proceed slowly and do not read it light-heartedly, nor pass things over without thought. If you read and meditate with care and without haste, you will find your heart kindled and stirred by divine love to such a degree that you will consider all kinds of hardships and troubles to be a great consolation, and will even deem yourself unworthy to suffer such tribulations.

What is more, if you receive any praise or benefit because of some talent God has bestowed upon you, you will not be puffed up with pride and exalt yourself, for if you read the Book of Life you will understand that your talents have not been given to you because of any merit of your own. This is one of the signs by which a person may know that the grace of God is in him: he will not become inflated with pride, nor haughty about his gifts, but will always remain humble.

You must know therefore that this Book of Life is nothing else but Jesus Christ, the Son of God, the Incarnate Word and Wisdom of the Father. His life is an example and a pattern to every human person who wishes to be saved. It is right that the members of the body, the Church, should follow the same road that has been taken by the Head.

CHAPTER THIRTY-ONE

Christ's Acceptance of Suffering and Our Reluctance to Suffer

Angela enumerates some of Christ's sufferings and laments our reluctance to bear hardships. She counsels her disciples to endure adversity with patience.

Jesus Christ, the true Book of Life, endured innumerable sufferings from the time of his birth to his death on the cross. At his birth he was not cradled upon feathers, but laid upon straw in a stable and in a hard manger. As a young and tender infant he was driven out of his country into Egypt and wandered forth with his mother, the sweet and gentle Virgin, and with the aged Joseph.

When he was a man he went into the desert and fasted forty days and forty nights, enduring hunger, thirst and temptations of the devil. He travelled through villages, hamlets and cities of Palestine, suffering heat and bitter cold, sweat and weariness, and at the last, torture and a bitter death. No tongue can tell nor heart imagine the sufferings he underwent at the time of his Passion. He was sold into the hands of his enemies. He was betrayed, denied, forsaken, accused and reviled, judged and condemned and led like a thief to the cross, stripped of his clothes, done to death and pierced with a spear. Thus Jesus died and thus men accomplished their evil deed. By the pain he endured he saved us from sin, reconciling us to the Father and opening the gates of Paradise.

How incredible is the goodness which God has shown towards us. He made grace to abound where sin had abounded.[1] Truly he has shown us the right road that we should follow. Yet we resist the sufferings that come upon us, wretched sinners that we are. We flee them, reject them, murmur bitterly against them and eagerly seek consolations and remedies by which we may be relieved of them. We not only seek to escape from worldly pains and afflictions, which might save us and purge us of sin, but we refuse the assistance of our most wise and holy physician, Jesus Christ.

If God, in his wisdom, ordains that it should be a little cold, we immediately draw near to the fire and cover ourselves with many clothes. And if it happens to be scorching hot, we seek the cold and see how we may cool ourselves. If our head or our stomach aches, we weep and sigh and run off to the doctor to seek remedies. We lie comfortably and softly in bed, eat dainty foods, and to relieve our pain we weary God and the saints by our constant prayers, vows and promises to fast, to go on pilgrimages and other such things. But we do not seek remedies for the sicknesses of our soul and the remission of our sins.

What a lot of things we do, and money we spend, in order to avert those pains, afflictions and adversities, which God in his mercy either sends us or allows to befall us! It is better to wait upon God and endure patiently what he sends, for he is the heavenly physician, who sends adversity to purge and discipline us, to teach us and to perfect our soul. We like to choose the kind of afflictions we can bear, but those which we are forced to bear against our will are those which are sent by divine providence and should be borne with patience and willingness.

Therefore I advise you, my children, to endure cold and heat and scorching weather, pains in the head or the stomach or other parts of the body. Do not be curious about finding remedies, except in urgent necessity and for the proper maintenance of bodily health, for this only hinders the good of the soul. I say to you moreover that when God orders or allows us to suffer poverty, oppression, persecution, shame and the death of friends, we should not be sorry for ourselves, but bear them patiently and accept them willingly and gladly for his sake and for the good of our souls. How can a miserable soul who is always seeking consolations in this world approach him who is the Way and our example in suffering? Truly the Son of God has been given to us as a pattern and example, as

---

[1] "Where sin abounded, grace did abound more exceedingly." Romans 5:20.

a teacher and a master, so that we might learn to despise the glory of this world and its shallow comforts.

Tribulation is exceedingly profitable to us, so let us not try to avoid it, or be alarmed by it. I say to you with all my heart and with absolute certainty that it is precisely these holy and precious trials and tribulations which bring us to heaven. It is through poverty, tears, suffering and persecution that the joys of eternity are obtained. I believe that nothing helps us as much as tribulation in the living of a good life.[2] Therefore may God illuminate us in our troubles, and may he comfort and console us when we suffer and may his name be glorified for ever.

[2] "Let us also rejoice in our tribulations, knowing that tribulation worketh patience." Romans 5:3.

CHAPTER THIRTY-TWO

We Should Serve God Without Looking for a Reward

The service of God and the knowledge that we are doing his will is its own reward. Angela warns her pupils against service which is undertaken for the sake of spiritual consolations.

We should not always be thinking of the consolations we receive from serving God. Is it possible do you suppose that Mary, the mother of Jesus, when she saw her beloved son on the cross crying aloud and dying, asked for spiritual consolation for herself in that hour? Indeed no. She accepted the grief and anguish which came to her because of her son's death. We too should share in the suffering of the cross. It is a sign of little love and great presumption if we wish to share in Christ's joy without sharing in his pain.

Those who serve God for the sake of reaping spiritual rewards, whose souls are fat and full of sweetness, do not acquire as much merit as those who run to God and serve him without any consolation. The divine light which proceeds from the life of Christ instructs us concerning the way by which we may reach God and be in God, namely the road on which Jesus Christ himself walked, the road of suffering.

Come my children, hasten to the cross of Christ. Take his pain, contempt and poverty upon yourselves and enter fervently into his Passion, for he loved us, and for love's sake he was willing to die for us. He did this that he might redeem us and furnish us with an example of how we should bear hard things for love of him. You, then, must be faithful to him, for he is faithful to you. The soul is bound to adore him for himself, for he is worthy to be loved and served by everyone because of his surpassing goodness.

Glory, therefore, be to God omnipotent, who has called us into being, and fashioned us in his own image. Honour, glory and power be to him, the all-merciful, for it has pleased him to redeem us and to exalt us to himself. Praise and glory be to our most sweet God, who by his unfailing goodness has given us his kingdom and brought us into fellowship with himself.

CHAPTER THIRTY-THREE

Three Kinds of Prayer

Angela names three kinds of prayer: corporal, mental and supernatural, which in traditional devotional language are termed vocal, mental and contemplative. By practising these kinds of prayer human persons are brought to a knowledge and love of God.

It is by means of prayer, when we are actually praying, that we find God. There are three principal types of prayer: corporal, mental and supernatural. Corporal prayer is that which is accompanied by the uttering of words and by bodily actions such as bowing down, kneeling, asking for forgiveness.[1] I myself continually perform this kind of prayer which must be done attentively. For example when we say the Our Father we must think carefully about what we are saying and not repeat it hurriedly and in a meaningless fashion. Corporal prayer, said slowly and thoughtfully, may lead to mental prayer.

Mental prayer consists of meditation on God or the life of Jesus, and in this kind of prayer God floods the mind so completely that all other thoughts are dispelled from the mind. The tongue is prevented from doing its appointed task and cannot speak, for so completely is the mind filled with God that it cannot concern itself with anything else. Supernatural prayer may then follow from mental prayer.

Supernatural prayer is that in which the soul is so exalted by the meditation that it is uplifted above its own nature, and perceives more of God than it could do naturally. It is granted a supernatural understanding

1 The traditional aspects of vocal prayer are penitence, praise, thanksgiving, intercession and petition.

of God, although it cannot explain what it knows and perceives because it is above human reason and transcends its own nature.

In these three degrees of prayer human beings learn to know God and to know themselves. And knowing God, they love him, and loving him they desire to possess him. The divine wisdom has ordained that no one should attain to mental prayer who has not previously exercised himself in corporal prayer. Nor does the Divine Wisdom allow anyone to attain to supernatural prayer who has not first engaged in both corporal and mental prayer.

When we pray we must keep our whole heart fixed on what we are doing, for if our heart is divided we lose the fruit of true prayer. In all other actions, like eating and drinking, it is not necessary for us to have such single-mindedness. The reason why we are tempted during prayer is because our heart is not given wholly to God. Jesus taught us by his deeds and words to pray. He truly loves us and desires our good. He said, "Ask and you will receive," and to his disciples he said, "Watch and pray that you may not enter into temptation."[2] In many parts of the Gospel you will find that he instructs us to pray, and he regards prayer as a precious and sacred activity. He himself prayed at the time of his Passion and said, "Father, if it be possible, let this cup pass from me; nevertheless not my will but thine by done."[3] Always keep this example of prayer before you, my dear children, and see that you follow it closely.

[2] Matthew 26:41.
[3] Luke 22:42.

CHAPTER THIRTY-FOUR

Obedience to the Will of God

Angela advises one of her pupils to study the life of Christ, to follow his example in obeying God's will, to examine his conscience, to repent of his sins and to persevere in prayer.

You see therefore that when Jesus prayed he submitted his will to the will of the Father. You, then, my dear son, must follow his example. Afterwards, as he hung on the cross, he prayed, "Father, into your hands I commit my spirit." What more can I say except that his whole life was a prayer, utterly dedicated to God and perfectly manifesting God in all he said and did. Why then are you neglectful regarding your prayers, since nothing is obtained without prayer? If Christ, who was true God as well as true man, found it necessary to pray and did not accept anything without prayer, how dare you, a miserable creature, hope to receive anything without prayer?

First you must study the Book of Life, that is the life and teaching of Christ. You will profit much by doing this, but as you learn to live in Christ and follow his example, you will be troubled by many temptations of the world, the flesh and the devil. If you want to overcome these trials and temptations you must pray, and begin by purifying yourself in mind and body. Think carefully of all the evil you have done. Examine the motives and intentions behind your good deeds, your works of mercy, your prayers, tears and fastings, and reflect on how remiss you have been in doing God's work, and how imperfectly you have performed those good deeds which you have done. Consider on the other hand how diligent you have been to do evil. Be ready to acknowledge your sins and to be sorry for them and to confess them.

Then by contrition and confession your soul will be cleansed and you will be like the publican of the parable who prayed, "Lord, be merciful to me a sinner."[1] Then by your prayers you will be enlightened.

[1] Luke 18:9–14.

CHAPTER THIRTY-FIVE

The Greater the Temptation the Greater the Need to Pray

Temptation must be resisted by constant and fervent prayer. Prayer will enlighten and humble the soul. Satan tries to lure us from the path of truth and virtue, but Christ has lovingly redeemed us by his suffering and death.

Watch and pray so that you do not give any advantage to the enemy who is continually around you.[1] When you cease to pray you give an opportunity to the devil. The more you are tempted the more you must persevere in prayer. Sometimes, however, prayer itself may be the occasion of temptation, for the demons are opposed to prayer and endeavour by every means to hinder you. But pay no attenion to anything except the prayers, and in this way you will be freed from your temptation. Through prayer you will be enlightened, purified and united to God. In prayer God manifests himself to you and shows you yourself as you are. This manifestation of God and the self issues in humility, and the more the soul is humbled by the action of divine grace upon it, the more that same grace increases in us, springing afresh out of the depths of humility. And the more that grace increases in the soul, the more the soul abases itself, prostrating itself in true humility.

Man's perfection consists in knowing the greatness of God and his own nothingness. We have already said that a person attains to this by

[1] "Be sober, be watchful, for your adversary the devil, as a roaring lion, walketh about, seeking whom he may devour." 1 Peter 5:8.

gazing at Jesus Christ, the Book of Life, and by modelling his or her life on him. Therefore, my son, have done with slothfulness and negligence. I urge you to watch and pray, and do not neglect the performance of good works, especially when you are deprived of any fervour in your devotions. When it happens that God withdraws all warmth and fervour from you, whether because of your own fault, or because God wants to strengthen your faith, do continue to watch and pray and to perform good works as before. And if trials and temptations befall you, by which you are purged and purified, do submit to them humbly and be faithful in prayers, vigils, tears and urgent requests to God. Then God, in his mercy, will give you back your warmth and fervour. Do your part and God will certainly do his. Try to see the beginning, the middle and the end of the road where the Spirit is leading you, and follow it only insofar as it coincides with the Book of Life, Jesus Christ. Be wary of those who claim to have the spirit of liberty, yet who openly oppose the Book of Life, the life and teaching of Christ, which is written according to the law.[2]

Satan, the seducer and murderer of our human race, is ever trying to lure us from the straight path, but Christ, true God and true man, has triumphed over him on the cross and saved us from his power. God, the Father, willed that his Son should suffer the pains of death and the torments of the cross rather than that the sins of the human race should remain unatoned for. Neither we ourselves, nor any other creature, could have made sufficient satisfaction and atonement for our sins. With great care, diligence and love Christ saved us and brought us back to the Father and to eternal happiness and fellowship with him. By this way alone are sinners saved. Therefore glory be to Jesus for ever and ever.

[2] The adherents of the heretical sect of the Free Spirit tended to regard themselves as above the law and the teachings and sacraments of the Church, with the result that they were often suspected of immorality. See R. E. Lerner, *The Heresy of the Free Spirit in the Later Middle Ages*. California Press. Also Fiona Bowie, *Beguine Spirituality*. SPCK, 1989.

CHAPTER THIRTY-SIX

The Humility and Example of Christ

The teaching and example of Christ is a lesson in humility. Individual human beings should be humble before God, their Creator, and humble before their fellow creatures, who are, or may be, in the same plight as themselves.

All prayer is worthless without humility, for humility is the special virtue most needful to man. Look then my children at the example of humility provided by Christ crucified and you will see perfect humility. Look at his life and listen to his teaching. What he taught he also practised, and all was done with the marvellous virtue of humility. Endeavour with your whole mind and energy to follow in his steps. He was in the form of God, yet he laid aside his divine nature and took upon himself the form of a servant, humbling himself and being obedient, even to death on the cross.[1] Truly he offers himself to us as a model of humility, counselling us to take heed to ourselves. "Learn from me, for I am meek and lowly of heart", he said.[2] So pay attention, my dear sons, to his teaching and reflect on its profundity, value and beauty.

On another occasion he set us an example in humility when he washed his disciples' feet, and he told us to imitate him. He said, "If I, your Lord and Master, have washed your feet, you also ought to wash one another's feet. I have given you an example, that you should do as I have done to you. Indeed, I say to you, a servant is not greater than his lord . . . If you know these things, happy are you if you do them."[3]

[1] Philippians 2:5–9; 2 Matthew 11:29.
[2] Matthew 11:29.
[3] John 13:12–17.

The saviour of the world has shown us that meekness and lowliness of heart is the root and foundation of all virtues. Neither abstinence, nor fasting, nor hardship, nor poverty, nor the wearing of rough clothing, nor the outward show of good works, nor the performing of miracles can avail anything without humility. So precious is this virtue, and so firm its foundation, that the Lord particularly desired that we should learn it from him, for the whole perfection of the spiritual life is built upon it.

This lowliness of heart which Christ wished to teach us brings with it a certain marvellous and clear light which animates the soul and imparts to it a discernment of its own nothingness and the immensity of the divine goodness. When a person knows himself to be nothing, and devoid of all goodness, he will give praise to God, the omnipotent being, and he will pray to him with greater earnestness.

The greatest and chief of all virtues is love, that is love for God and love for one's neighbour.[4] This love springs from that light of which I have just spoken, for when the soul perceives that it is nothing, and that God has inclined himself to such vile nothingness and united himself to it (i.e. the soul), then the soul burns fervently with love for him.[5] Through this love the soul is made one with God.

The soul that is transformed like this, through the love of its Creator, then loves all creatures who are created by him. It perceives God in all his creatures and sees how greatly he loves them. The soul rejoices at this, and rejoices too at the good fortune of its neighbour, and being kindly disposed towards its neighbour, it grieves and laments at his ill fortune, and does not presume to judge or despise him when such ill fortune befalls him. The reason for this is that once the soul has been illuminated by the light we have spoken of, it immediately looks to itself, and knows that it is in as bad a plight as its neighbour, or even worse. It knows that if it has not fallen into sin, it is because it has been helped by God's grace which has upheld it and strengthened it and protected it against evil and temptation.

Therefore the soul judges no one, but rather humbles itself all the more, for seeing the sins and defects of its neighbour, it looks to itself and

---

[4] Matthew 22:37–40.
[5] I.e., because God, in his greatness, power and perfection, condescends to man in his littleness, sin and imperfection.

understands clearly that if it had not been upheld by God, it would have fallen into those same sins into which its neighbour had fallen, and even more readily. Thus perceiving that it has no power of itself to achieve any good, it puts its whole trust and hope in God.

I say therefore that you must hold firmly to this virtue of humility. Then you will not be so inclined to strife and contention. You will be like those who are deaf and do not hear, and like those who are dumb and do not speak. Those who are imbued with humility are calm, quiet, pleasing to God and full of grace. When they hear harsh and bitter things said against them they will give their accusers a short answer and speak only in a low voice, and will be ready to give way rather than to enter into an argument. The one who is humble does not regard himself superior to others. Instead he is concerned to see his own faults and wretchedness and to accuse and judge himself and to mend his ways.

CHAPTER THIRTY-SEVEN

True and False Love

Angela warns her spiritual children against the pit-falls of so-called 'love'. Wisdom, discretion, and circumspection are required in distinguishing between true and false love. Love for God should be examined for motives which may be rooted in selfishness. Spiritual love between persons may, if not guarded against, degenerate into carnal love.

Love is the greatest of all virtues, that is love for God and love for one's neighbour. Without it prayer is of little account, neither is it pleasing to God. In order to be convinced of this take heed to what Jesus said. 'If you bring your gift to the altar and remember that your brother has anything against you, leave your gift there at the altar, and first be reconciled to your brother.'[1] Prayer must be offered in the spirit of love. In the Lord's Prayer we are taught to ask for the forgiveness of our sins. 'Forgive us our trespasses as we forgive those who trespass against us.'[2] This means that our sins will be forgiven by God insofar as we forgive those who have committed injuries and offences against us. If we forgive others we shall be united to them in love.

You must know this, my children, that just as love encompasses all that is good and worthy, hatred encompasses all that is unworthy and evil. This is why I fear love more than anything in the world, for love reaches right into the soul, more than anything else, and floods the whole mind and heart. True love can so easily degenerate into false love. If the soul is not armed with wisdom and discretion to protect itself, it may easily

[1] Matthew 5:23–24.
[2] Matthew 6:9–15.

fall into sin and suffer destruction. I am not speaking here of a love which is obviously wrong and immoral which must be eschewed and shunned by everyone as a perilous and diabolical thing. I am speaking rather of a good and spiritual love, such as exists between the soul and God, or between one person and another. Such love, without the exercise of wisdom and restraint, may become inordinate and corrupt.

If the love which the soul has for God is stirred with undue and inordinate fervour and lacks discretion, it may cease altogether or be deceived. Unruly emotions and things which lack order and discipline are neither good nor healthy. There are many people who believe that they are filled with the love of God, whereas in reality they love that which is opposed to him. What they really love is the world, the flesh and the devil. For example a person may only love God because he thinks that God can save him from sickness, trouble or earthly dangers. He loves himself and God in a wrong and disorderly manner, putting himself first instead of putting God first. He makes a god of himself, and does not love God except for what he can get out of him. He also loves his family and relations for his own benefit and for the honour they bring to him. He loves saintly and spiritual people and associates with them because he thinks that in doing so he will give the appearance of being holy and virtuous himself. He does not really love them for their own sake and for their goodness. Love such as this is not pure and may end up in all kinds of vice and concupiscence.

There are some who want to possess knowledge, understanding and book-learning and the ability to converse about spiritual matters, not for the benefit and good of others, but that they themselves might be honoured and praised. They love to be "spiritual" so that they may be esteemed by others to be "spiritual". They love too to be poor, patient, obedient and outwardly humble and virtuous so that they may appear to others to be virtuous. They desire that no one should be as virtuous as they are, but in fact they are like Lucifer who wished no one to be equal to him. Pride is their greatest vice.

There are some who love religious and devout people who come among them. Nevertheless their love sometimes grows too powerful and if it is not tempered with discipline and restraint, it becomes evil, and even turns to carnal love. Their hearts become united in an unwholesome bond and they waste their time in harmful and unprofitable conversation.

Those who are a prey to this kind of love always want the person they love to be present and they become sick if he or she is not present. If the beloved person is there, the love increases, and what pleases the one pleases the other, and what displeases the one displeases the other. Therefore if the soul is not strong enough to control the ardour of this love, and if it lacks discipline and discretion, it deteriorates into a disordered kind of love.

And if, when this disorder sets in, the loved person also lacks discretion, and is in the same way wounded by the dart of love, then they have reached a more dangerous stage in their love, for they begin to disclose their secrets to one another, and say, among other things, how much they love each other. They say, "There is no one in all the world whom I love as much as I love you and no one else who lives so completely in my heart." These and many other things they say, because they are compelled to speak about what they feel. Thus they continue to want to love each other for the sake of 'spiritual devotion' and for the supposed spiritual benefit they think they are deriving from such a love. But they are in grave danger of being tempted to unlawful behaviour. At first, reason dissuades them from such behaviour, for up till now, reason has prevailed and has not been entirely overcome by emotion and love. But soon love increases and reason decreases. The spirit becomes weak and the mind is darkened. They begin to believe that it is not sinful, and in no way harmful to the soul, if they touch one another. So they allow this to happen and begin to do wrong. Little by little they fall from their state of innocence and perfection, because reason has been obscured by love.

Then gradually as the power of reason begins to diminish they start to think that those dangerous things are nothing. They say "It is all right for us to do this, for it is not such a great sin, and we mean no evil." Thus, slowly those things which are unlawful come to be considered lawful, and love increases more and more, each submitting entirely to the will of the other, each doing what the other wants and not opposing it for any reason to the contrary. Hence it follows that love obtains all that it desires. And because of the lack of wisdom and discretion each is unable to refuse what the other invites him or her to do.

Then they begin to give up prayer, abstinence, solitude and all other virtues which they used to practise, attempting to imitate divine love by the most miserable worldly and carnal love. Sometimes their love increases to such a degree that neither the words nor the presence of the beloved give the satisfaction they did at first. But as they love more ardently, each wanting to know whether the beloved is wounded by the dart of love as deeply as the other, then it is that they fall into the greatest peril, both lover and beloved being inclined to sin.

For this reason I say that I fear love more than anything else, for in the name of 'love' all kinds of evil is committed, so be wary of it as you would be of a serpent, because good love between one person and another can so easily turn to evil love in the manner I have described.[3]

Know this, my children that the love of God constrains us to follow in the way of the cross. This is the sign that true love is working in us. Such love does not behave itself in an unseemly manner in eating and drinking and such like, nor does it exhibit a false kind of joy which says, 'I am under no law'. Instead it always subjects itself to the law of God. And when love has followed in the way of the cross to the utmost of its power, it will not boast, but still perceive itself to be unprofitable and not working according to the truth. It will see God as all love and itself as all unworthy and sinful.

[3] Again Angela may have had in mind the heresy of the Free Spirit, and been warning her disciples against its more extreme expressions, such as the promotion of free love.

CHAPTER THIRTY-EIGHT

How it may be Known that God has Entered the Soul

Though it could be argued that God is never absent from the human soul, even though his presence may not be discerned, nevertheless there are times when he seems to invade the soul and make his presence vividly felt, as Angela describes in this revelation.

God sometimes comes into the soul when one has neither called upon him nor prayed to him. He suddenly instils the soul with a warmth and love and sweetness which it does not feel in the normal way. This causes the soul to rejoice and to believe that this is the work of God himself who is present in the soul. Though the soul cannot see God within itself, it perceives that his grace is there, and this brings great joy to the soul.

The soul has a further sense of God being present when it hears the most sweet words being spoken to it, and its joy is greatly increased. I myself affirm that the soul feels the presence of God with a marvellous understanding and a love so fervent and intense that it loses all love and concern for itself and for the body. It knows and understands and speaks about things which it has never been told by any human being before. The soul's understanding is greatly illuminated, and it only holds its peace with difficulty. If it does refrain from speaking, it does so because of the abundance of zeal and fervour it feels.

When one has a feeling of certainty that God dwells in the soul, there is also given to one a state of mind so perfect that it concurs entirely and truly with the soul in everything. The body and all its parts also agree in every way with the soul, and are in harmony with the soul, and together with it form one intention and one purpose.[1] Nor do the different parts of the body, with their desires and capacities, rebel against the will of the soul. They perfectly desire those things that are of God, though they had not hitherto desired them in any way. By grace the soul perceives that the Divine Being has entered into it and given it a desire for God and the things of God. The soul then feels that God is mingled with it and has made friends with it.

Furthermore when God comes into the soul it is sometimes granted to the soul to see God. It sees him without any bodily shape or form, yet more clearly than one person sees another. The eyes of the soul see a spiritual presence and not a bodily one. I am not able to speak of this because words fail me. But it is indeed true that the soul rejoices at that sight with an ineffable joy, and it sees nothing else, for it is this which fills it with the most inestimable satisfaction. This searching and beholding of God is so profound that it grieves me not to be able to describe anything of it whatsoever, since it is not something that can be imagined, or touched or estimated.

The soul knows in many ways that God has entered into it, but I will speak here of only two ways. The first is that a holy unction and calm suffuses the soul and revives it, and subdues all the parts of the body, so that they are in harmony with the soul. It hears God speaking within it and feels his presence, and because of this indescribable calm, the soul knows with absolute certainty that he is present. It saddens me that I can find no adequate words to describe this sweet unction and holy calm which fills the soul.

The second way by which one may know that God is in the soul is by the embrace that God gives to the soul. No father or mother or son or any other person at all can embrace a beloved person with so great a love as that with which God embraces the soul. He draws it to himself with such sweetness and gentleness, that I think there is no one in the world who could tell of it, or express it, or believe it, unless he himself has experienced it. He might perhaps perceive something of this love, yet he could not possibly know it as it truly is. I am quite sure of this, that God implants in the soul a most sweet love, which makes it burn for

[1] She is speaking here of that perfect integration and harmony of the whole personality; mind, body and soul, which flows from union with God, God in the person and the person in God.

Christ alone, and it brings with it so intense a light, that the soul understands the fullness of God's goodness.

The soul does not shed tears anymore, whether tears of joy or sorrow or any other kind, for when the soul has tears, it is in a lower state. God pours such a profusion of sweetness into the soul that it can ask no more. Indeed if this were to endure it would be in paradise itself.

When the soul is assured of God and refreshed by his presence, the body also receives health, satisfaction and nobility, and is refreshed like the soul, though to a lesser degree. The reason (mind) and the soul, being thus refreshed and reinvigorated by God, address the body and the senses in this manner: "See how great the benefits are that God has bestowed upon you, the body and the senses, through me, the mind and spirit! If you will only obey me and submit to me, you will profit thereby. Consider the numerous advantages which you and I have already lost because you, the body, have not been obedient to me, the mind and spirit. You have behaved contrary to my wishes and in future must be obedient to God."

At once the body will submit itself to the soul, and the senses will submit to the reason, realising how profoundly they can share in the pleasures and delights of the soul. Then the body says, "Hitherto my pleasures have been base and physical because I am the body. But you, the mind and soul, are of great nobility and are able to enjoy divine and heavenly pleasures." Thus the body laments against the soul, and the senses against reason, perceiving that the pleasures of the soul are immensely more sublime than the body had imagined. So then the body submits to the soul and is obedient in everything.[2]

I was not always able to conceal from my companion and from the others I mixed with, the state I was in and the spiritual ecstasies I experienced, for these affected my body, and at times my face was all resplendent and my eyes shone like candles. But at other times, depending on how the visions varied, I was as pale as death. Sometimes

[2] Here Angela is enunciating the perennial conflict which exists in human nature between flesh and spirit, and the necessity to bring the flesh in subjection and obedience to the mind and spirit. St Paul writes "Walk by the Spirit, and you will not fulfil the lusts of the flesh. For the flesh lusts against the Spirit, and the Spirit against the flesh, for these are contrary the one to the other." Galatians 5:16–17.

my joy would endure for many days, and some of the joys were so complete and perfect that I think I shall never lose them, and when sadness comes upon me I instantly recall those joys and then I am in no way troubled.

When I reflect within myself I sometimes perceive very vividly that those people who know God best are those who presume to speak of him the least, since he is infinite and inexpressible. They know that all they can possibly say of him is as nothing compared to what he truly is. God is so much greater than man's mind that man is unable even to think or speak of him. I believe that all that has ever been said about God, either in speech or in writing, from the time the world began, has in no way described the true nature of the Divine Being and his goodness. It is like half of a millet seed compared to the whole world.

CHAPTER THIRTY-NINE

Visions and Consolations

Visions are not to be demanded, but should be accepted when they are given. They enable one to see everything in perspective, and to know that all things derive from God, the Supreme Being.

God sometimes favours the soul by giving it marvellous visions and consolations. These must not be demanded of God, but neither must they be refused if he chooses to send them, for they draw the soul nearer to God, restoring, invigorating and uplifting it, so that it is stirred to look for and long to be united with its beloved, that is God. In this state the soul is contented because of the consolations. But when it is deprived of them, love stirs afresh in the soul and begins to seek for God himself. Only when the soul is united with God does it become stable and orderly and filled with a marvellous wisdom and maturity. It is so strengthened because of the love it has for the beloved that it would willingly die for him.

Then the soul considers its former state and all that it had been before as nothing compared to what it is now. It is concerned with nothing that is created and does not care about sickness or death, honour or disgrace. It is at peace and full of comfort and contentment and nothing can disturb it. It has lost all desire and cannot work, for when it beholds the visions I have spoken of, it cannot do anything whatsoever.

But no one in this present life is permitted to have these visions all the time, and when they cease, the soul is given a new and ardent desire to perform works of penitence. The love which is now kindled in the heart is more perfect than before, and makes the loving soul want to imitate its beloved, that is Christ crucified, whose sufferings lasted all the time he was on earth. Suffering marked the beginning of his life and continued to the end. He was always on the cross, a cross of poverty, grief and contempt. Whoever loves Jesus Christ, who was both God and man, will endeavour to transform himself into his likeness, following his example and doing that which he believes will be pleasing to him, and avoiding those things which displease him.[1]

When the soul sees the vision of God it perceives also that all creatures have their being from the Supreme Being, and that nothing exists which is not derived from him. It sees too that everything God made is good.[2] This vision of the Supreme Being awakens in the soul a love corresponding to itself and incites us to love everything that has been created by him. When the soul finds the Supreme Being yearning towards his creatures with love for them, then the soul yearns with love towards them too.

Those who are the true friends of God demonstrate their friendship by following his Son and keeping the eyes of their mind constantly fixed upon him. As for me, when I see him I desire never to depart from him, but to draw nearer to him. The more I remember him, the less I can speak of him and my tongue is tied. The joy which I have in those hands and feet is beyond my power to tell. To him be glory and honour for ever and ever.

[1] "If you love me, you will keep my commandments." John 14:15.
[2] "God saw everything that he had made, and, behold, it was very good." Genesis 1:31.

CHAPTER FORTY

The Way to Find God

We find God by praying and by giving our whole selves to him, and by conforming ourselves to the likeness of Christ.

The way to find God and to love him is by constant, devout and diligent prayer, and by reading the Book of Life, which provides us with a knowledge of God. We need to have a knowledge of God in order to love him, and that knowledge is to be found in Jesus Christ. Let us see to it, my dearest children, that we love God and are wholly transformed in him. Jesus Christ, who is God incarnate, is all love. He loves everyone and desires to be wholly loved by us.

You are God's spiritual children, chosen because of his love for you. It is true that we are all sons and daughters of God by creation, but he takes a special pleasure in you whom he has chosen and in whom he has implanted his love.[1] He finds his own likeness in you, a likeness formed solely by his grace and perfect love. The person who has genuinely changed his or her behaviour and manner of life so as to conform to the likeness of Christ is already on the way to perfection.

God, whose nature is good and noble, desires to possess the whole heart of his children and not only part of their heart. He does not wish anything to hinder his children in giving their heart to him. Yet he is so gracious and merciful that if we give him only a part he accepts it gladly, though his perfect love naturally longs for the whole and not just a part. We know that a bridegroom who loves his bride cannot bear that she

---

[1] Here she is specifically addressing her disciples, those devoted to the Franciscan way of life, friars and members of the Third Order.

should have any other companion except himself, either openly or secretly. Neither can God with the children he loves. He wishes to win our whole-hearted love and devotion.

If any person were to understand and taste the divine love in all its fullness, he would give himself entirely to God and would forsake all other creatures and indeed his very self for the sake of this Supreme Love.[2] Therefore if the soul wishes to attain this perfection of love, which requires the devotion of the whole self, then it must enter by the straight way and must walk on it with the feet of pure love, upright, orderly and fervent. It must not seek to love and serve God for the sake of a reward, but for his own sake, since God is good and worthy to be loved for himself. He was made man and was crucified for us.

[2] See Luke 14:25–27 which, as we have already observed, contains an injunction central to Angela's thought and behaviour.

CHAPTER FORTY-ONE

The Benefits of Tribulation

She speaks of the value of tribulation which is spiritually profitable and draws us closer to God.

Three benefits proceed from holy tribulation. First it converts us to God, and being thus converted, it draws us closer to him. Secondly, it makes us grow in the spirit, for just as good soil, well prepared, sends out shoots and bears fruit when the rain falls upon it, so also the soul grows in virtue when tribulation befalls it. Thirdly, it gives comfort and peace, rest and tranquility.

Holy tribulation is exceedingly profitable to us, so let us not try to avoid it or be alarmed by it. I say to you with all my heart and with absolute certainty that it is precisely these holy and precious sufferings by which we purchase the kingdom of heaven. It is through poverty and tears, suffering and persecution that the joys of eternity are obtained. We do not know their worth. They are our noblest advocates and truest witnesses which will be most readily believed in the presence of God.

I believe that nothing helps us as much as tribulation in the living of a good life. For this reason I could say that I am envious of those who are troubled. It is certain, my sons, that if the true benefit and value of tribulation were known, we would thieve tribulation from one another, as if it were something to be coveted. May God illuminate us in our troubles, and may he comfort and console us when we suffer, and may his name be glorified for ever.

CHAPTER FORTY-TWO

The Eucharist

Angela reflects on various facets of the Eucharist, the sacrament by which Christ's presence is known to his followers, and by which he is united to them.

The Eucharist is the sacrament of grace and love which stirs us to devout prayer and bestows on us humility of heart and leads us to all goodness. I am certain that no one who earnestly contemplates this holy mystery will be insensitive to the love which inspired it. Once this has been understood the soul itself is filled with love and gratitude.

This holy mystery is something new and marvellous above everything else and far beyond our human comprehension. Although it was first celebrated by Christ many years ago, as is explained in Scripture, nevertheless it is ever new as regards its re-enactment, and ever imparts to those who receive it in repentance and faith, new grace and power. There are many graces and virtues which the sacrament accomplishes in God's chosen ones, but we shall not marvel too much at what the sacrament accomplishes if we remember the mighty power of him who does them. Nor shall we wonder at how the sacrament of Christ's body and blood can be present on numerous altars at the same time, here and in other places, on this side of the ocean and upon that. Though we cannot fully understand this mystery we must believe and not doubt, for nothing is impossible to God.

It was because of his boundless love that he instituted this sacrament and entered into it and will abide in it until the end of the world. By means of this sacrament we not only commemorate Christ's death, but we are assured of his perpetual closeness to us. He instituted this sacrament so that after his death he might always be united with us, for love always unites the lover and the beloved. Contemplating this love, surely there can be no one so hard-hearted and indifferent that he would not feel moved to return the love of such a lover as Jesus Christ. The Eucharist is a proper memorial of his bitter Passion and the shedding of his blood for us wretched sinners. What soul is there who, contemplating his sufferings, is not encouraged to bear suffering for his sake?

The sacrament of the Eucharist raises us up to heavenly things. It was ordained by the Holy Trinity that the Holy Trinity might bind itself to that which It loves above all else, that is the soul of human beings. The sacrament draws the soul to God and away from all created things, uniting the soul with the uncreated God. It bestows divine love upon the soul and purifies it of all its sins. It was ordained by the Holy Trinity that the Holy Trinity might unite and incorporate Itself with us, and us with It. The Trinity desires that we should receive the sacrament so that the Trinity may receive us, and that we should bear It, so that It should bear us and fortify and comfort us.

To those who repent, the forgivness of sins is granted through the sacrament, and strength is given to resist temptation. Many other gifts and benefits are conferred upon us if we receive the sacrament worthily and are not hindered by our misdeeds. So whoever intends to come to this holy sacrament should consider who he is coming to, how he should come and why. He comes for a certain good thing, which is itself all good, and the cause of all good, that is God, the maker and giver and possessor of all good. God himself is the only good, and without him there can be no other good. This good suffices and fills everything. In this sacrament man comes to receive this good thing, which is God made man, in whom everything exists and who is above all things. May you who are the Supreme God, unknown by many, unheeded and unloved, make yourself known to those of us who, with our whole heart, desire you.

All the angels and saints rejoice with Christ in this holy mystery, for that which pleases Christ, pleases them also. Christ rejoices to be with the children of men in this sacrament, and all the blessed ones in the Church triumphant rejoice when those in the Church on earth receive this holy food. Therefore the whole Church rejoices and praises God for all his benefits and blessings and give him thanks for his goodness.

CHAPTER FORTY-THREE

Angela's Last Piece of Writing

This is part of the last piece of writing which Angela accompished before her death in January 1309. Dictating to her scribe she spoke the following words:

O Lord Jesus Christ, make me worthy to understand the profound mystery of your holy incarnation, which you have worked for our sake and for our salvation. Truly there is nothing so great and wonderful as this, that you, my God, who are the creator of all things, should become a creature, so that we should become like God. You have humbled yourself and made yourself small that we might be made mighty. You have taken the form of a servant, so that you might confer upon us a royal and divine beauty.

You, who are beyond our understanding, have made yourself understandable to us in Jesus Christ. You, who are the uncreated God, have made yourself a creature for us. You, who are the untouchable One, have made yourself touchable to us. You, who are most high, make us capable of understanding your amazing love and the wonderful things you have done for us. Make us able to understand the mystery of your incarnation, the mystery of your life, example and doctrine, the mystery of your cross and Passion, the mystery of your resurrection and ascension.

Blessed are you, O Lord, for coming to earth as a man. You were born that you might die, and in dying that you might procure our salvation. O marvellous and indescribable love! In you is all sweetness and joy! To contemplate your love is to exalt the soul above the world and to enable it to abide alone in joy and rest and tranquility.

Lord, give us grace to understand your supreme love in creating and redeeming us, in choosing the human race from all eternity to attain to a vision of yourself. Give us grace to understand your goodness in creating us with the gift of reason, by which we may perceive your glory and our own sin and wretchedness, and by which we are able to resist our sensual nature which inclines us to sin. You have created us, Lord, in your own likeness and clothed us with the light of reason. O Supreme Being help us to understand your love, for you yourself are love! All the angels and saints love you and contemplate you and gaze upon you and worship you for ever. Amen.

CHAPTER FORTY-FOUR

Her Final Piece of Advice to her Spiritual Children

At about the time of the Feast of St Michael and All Angels (September 29) 1308, Angela became ill and knew her end was near. During the period between the commencement of her illness and her death in January 1309 she gave some special spiritual counsel to her followers. I give here only a short extract from one of her last discourses.

My beloved children I urge you to strive to be truly humble, not only in your outward behaviour, but in your innermost hearts, so that you may be true disciples of him who said, 'Learn from me, for I am gentle and humble of heart.'[1] Do not be concerned about power and honours or being preferred before others, but strive to be of no account and esteem yourself as nothing; then Christ will exalt you by his grace. Beware of worldly self-sufficiency in such things as honour, power and preferment, for they are very deceptive and lead to pride. But there is even greater deception in spiritual self-sufficiency and pride in such things as being able to speak eloquently of God, being able to understand the Scriptures and in performing great penances and such like. Therefore I say esteem yourselves as nothing.

See to it that you love one another, not only among yourselves but towards all people. Endeavour to cultivate this charity and do not judge anyone, even though you see people committing mortal sin. Certainly sin must always be displeasing to you and regarded with the greatest

---

[1] Matthew 11:29.

horror, but I say that you should not judge sinners, nor despise them. You do not know how God judges people. There are many who, according to human judgement, are worthy of hell, but who, according to the wisdom and judgement of God, are saved, and there are many who appear to us to be worthy of being saved, but who are deemed worthy of hell by God. There are some whom I feel sure God will bring back to his grace, but whom you have despised. God's judgements are not our judgements.

When Blessed Angela of Foligno had finished these sayings, she placed her hand on the head of each of her disciples and said, "May you be blessed by the Lord and by me, my children. I bless all of you who are here and those who are not present with us."

CHAPTER FORTY-FIVE

Angela's Death as Reported by her Disciples

Blessed Angela, our mother in Christ, died at about the time of Christmas. As she lay very sick she spoke the words, "The Word was made flesh." After a long silence, as though she were returning from another place, she said, "Every creature fails, and all that the angels understand is not sufficient to comprehend this." Then she added, "My soul is washed and cleansed in the blood of Jesus Christ."

After this she said, "Jesus Christ has now presented me to the Father and these words have been spoken to me: O bride and fair one, you are loved by me with a perfect love. Truly it is not my wish that you should come to me in the midst of such great suffering, but with rejoicing. It is fitting that a king should lead the bride whom he loves home, and clothe her with a royal robe."[1]

Then he showed me the robe, just as a bridegroom shows the robe to the bride whom he has loved for so long. It was neither of scarlet, nor of sendal, nor of samite, but was of a certain marvellous light which clothed the soul.[2] Then he showed me to the Bridegroom, the Eternal Word, and the Word suffused my soul and touched me throughout and embraced me and said, "Come, my love, my bride, beloved by me with true delight. Come! for all the saints await your coming with exceeding joy". He said again to me, "I will not give you into the care of the angels

---

[1] There are strong echoes here of the Song of Songs, a favourite scriptural source for medieval mystics and theologians, particularly St Bernard of Clairvaux.
[2] Sendal – a fine silk fabric used for clothing on ceremonial occasions in the Middle Ages. Samite – a heavy silk fabric interwoven with gold and silver threads.

and saints to lead you to me, but I will come myself and fetch you and raise you to myself, for you have made yourself ready and pleasing to me."

Now the day before Angela was near to death she often repeated the words, "Father, into your hands I commend my spirit".[3] Once after repeating the words she told us that she heard a voice saying to her, "It is impossible in death that you should lose that which has been impressed upon your heart in life."

On that same day all the pains she had been tormented with in her limbs ended. She lay in such repose of body and cheerfulnes of spirit that she appeared as though she had already tasted something of the joy that had been promised her. Indeed she told us that the joys of heaven were just beginning for her. She lay very joyfully in this quietness of body and cheerfulness of spirit until the hour of Compline on the Saturday, surrounded by many of the brothers who administered the sacraments to her. On that same day, on the Octave of the Holy Innocents, at the last hour, she gently fell asleep and rested in peace.[4] That most holy soul was set free from the flesh and was drawn into the abyss of the divine infinitude and received the garment of innocence and immortality from Christ, the heavenly Bridegroom. To that same place may he likewise bring us all by the virtue of his cross.

The venerable bride of Christ, Angela of Foligno, passed from the shipwreck of this world into the joys of heaven in the year of our Lord's Incarnation one thousand, three hundred and nine, on the fourth day of January in the time of Pope Clement the fifth.

---

[3] Jesus' last cry from the cross. Luke 23:46.
[4] I.e., on the final day of the Octave – 4th of January. Holy Innocents' Day at the beginning of the Octave is on 28th of December.

Further Reading

Medieval Mystics

Angela of Foligno. The Book of Divine Consolations. Tr. Mary Steegman. London, 1909.

Angela of Foligno. Complete Works. Ed. Paul Lachance. Paulist Press, 1993.

Birgitta of Sweden. Life & Selected Revelations. Tr. Albert Kezel. Paulist Press, 1990.

Catherina of Siena. The Dialogue. Tr. Suzanne Noffke. Paulist Press, 1980.

Cloud of Unknowing (Anon.). Tr. Clifton Wolters. London, 1961.

Francis of Assisi. Life. Little Flowers. Mirror of Perfection. Ed. Thomas Okey. London, 1941.

Jacopone da Todi. Lauds. Tr. S. and E. Hughes. London, 1982.

Julian of Norwich. Revelations of Divine Love. Tr. Clifton Wolters. London, 1966.

The Book of Margery Kempe. Tr. Barry Windeatt. London, 1985.

Porete, Marguerite. *A Mirror for Simple Souls.* Tr. Charles Crawford. Dublin, 1981.

Suso Henry: The Life of the Servant. Tr. James Clark. Cambridge, 1982.

Spirituality and the Church

Bowie, Fiona, *Beguine Spirituality.* London, 1989.

Dionysius the Areopagite. The Divine Names & The Mystical Theology. Tr. C. E. Rolt. London, 1940/1986.

Moorman, John, *A History of the Franciscan Movement.* Oxford, 1968.

Pretroff, E. A. *Medieval Women's Visionary Literature.* Oxford, 1986.

Southern, R. W. *Western Society and the Church in the Middle Ages.* London, 1970/1979.

Underhill, Evelyn. *Mysticism.* London, 1941/1993.

Underhill, Evelyn. *Mystics of the Church.* Cambridge, 1925/1975.

Walsh, James. *Spirituality Through the Centuries.* London, 1965.

PERSONAL NOTES

PERSONAL NOTES